GW00645221

RUGBY
TO
LOUGHBOROUGH

David Pearce

MP *Middleton Press*

Front cover: B1 4-6-0 No. 61206 leaves Belgrave & Birstall with the 09.30 Leicester to Nottingham local on a lovely summer's morning in August 1961. (G.D.King/Colour-Rail.com)

Back cover upper: A glorious day in June 1959 finds a time honoured engine change in progress at Leicester Central. V2 2-6-2 No. 60863 brews up in readiness for the off with an up express, having replaced the unidentified B1 4-6-0 standing in bay Platform 4 on the left. (J.B.McCann/Colour-Rail.com)

*Back cover lower: This view at Quorn & Woodhouse looking south from the station bridge carrying Forest Road over the railway offers D11 4-4-0 No. 62660 **Butler-Henderson** departing with a southbound train on the 24th February 1992. It is remarkable to think that scenes such as this could be repeated so many years after the station had been discarded from the national network. (D.C.Pearce)*

Published January 2012

ISBN 978 1 908174 12 3

© Middleton Press, 2012

Design Deborah Esher

Published by
>   *Middleton Press*
>   *Easebourne Lane*
>   *Midhurst*
>   *West Sussex*
>   *GU29 9AZ*
Tel: 01730 813169
Fax: 01730 812601
Email: info@middletonpress.co.uk
www.middletonpress.co.uk

Printed in the United Kingdom by Henry Ling Limited, at the Dorset Press, Dorchester, DT1 1HD

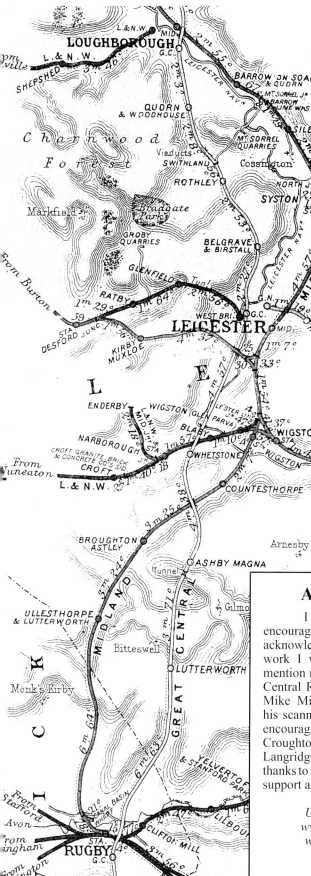

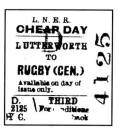

ACKNOWLEDGEMENTS

I am very grateful for the assistance and encouragement received from all the contributors acknowledged in the captions, but equally those whose work I was, regrettably, unable to include. Special mention must be made of fellow members of the Great Central Railway Society, particularly David Bodicoat, Mike Mitchell and Tony West, Michael Rhodes for his scanning skills, Richard Adderson for support and encouragement, not to mention a few tickets. Godfrey Croughton has supplied most of the latter and Norman Langridge has proof read the text. As always, special thanks to my wife, Suzy, and the boys for encouragement, support and putting up with my interests.

Useful websites - www.gcrsociety.co.uk
www.gcrleicester.info   www.tillyweb.biz
www.gcrailway.co.uk   www.rcts.org.uk

GEOGRAPHICAL SETTING

The market town of Rugby lies in the county of Warwickshire, on lias beds of glacial origin that form the scarplands of the South East Midlands. It is also situated at an important railway crossroads on one of the premier trunk routes between London and Scotland. By comparison with the London and North Western's West Coast Main Line the presence of the Great Central's London Extension was altogether a more modest affair though its northern approach was no less imposing.

As the line strikes north through the eastern suburbs of Rugby it gradually descends to cross the Avon Valley. In so doing it thrusts across the West Coast Main Line on an impressive girder bridge, followed by brick arches and embankments that, in turn, take it across the Oxford Canal, a waterway it has more or less kept company with since Braunston, and the River Avon itself. The viaducts, embankments, cuttings and occasional tunnels continue to characterise the line all the way to its industrial heartlands of the north.

Climbing out of the Avon Valley in a roughly north-easterly direction the line encounters another major trunk route as it crosses Watling Street, the Roman road now known more mundanely as the A5. Lying between Newton and Shawell, the road forms the county boundary as the line bids farewell to Warwickshire and enters Leicestershire.

Apart from a short dip near Lutterworth, accounted for by the River Swift, a tributary of the Avon, the line continues to climb through undulating countryside to a summit a couple of miles south of Ashby Magna. As it strikes more or less due north towards Leicester, a long sweeping descent of 1 in 176 (the London Extension's ruling grade) follows through a fairly sparsely populated area of the county. What the landscape lacks in populace and, to a certain extent, beauty, is made up for by agriculture and the rich pastures that sustain it. Two miles to the north of Ashby Magna the line crosses the Midland Counties (later Midland Railway) Rugby to Leicester line not far from Cosby. At the same time it leaves the lias behind here in favour of keuper marls that will feature all the way to the Trent Valley and beyond.

In its final years the GC was also joined by the M1, paralleling it to the east from Lutterworth to 'Cosby Corner' just south of Whetstone. Here the line crosses the M1 as it enters the flood plain of the River Soar. The gradient eases a little as the line crosses the valley of the Sence, a tributary of the Soar, on a viaduct followed by the Grand Union Canal. It also encounters the LNW's Leicester to Nuneaton line with which it had a physical connection during building and again during the First World War.

The River Soar and the Grand Union Canal accompany the line all the way through Leicester with the first crossing of the Soar at Aylestone. The line crosses the Soar no less than ten times during its passage through Leicestershire. The river and canal keep to the east side of the line approaching Leicester before taking a long sweep round to the west. As the line threads the suburbs approaching Leicester, it is crossed by the Midland Railway's Leicester to Burton line near to the GC's loco depot and goods facilities serving the city. The railway crosses the river and canal waters again just south of Central station on viaducts that carry the line almost all the way through the city. Indeed, it is the same viaduct that carries the line across the canal and, in turn, the Soar again a quarter of a mile to the north of the station. Here river, canal and railway part company for a while as the line climbs through Birstall before dropping down to Loughborough.

As the line descends through Rothley and crosses the waters of Swithland Reservoir it enters the ancient district of Charnwood Forest. The waters supply Leicester Corporation and the pastures, woodlands and pleasant uplands create a landscape famous for hunting. At Swithland an old mineral branch from Mountsorrel provided access to granite quarries to the east, quarries that were also linked to the Midland Main Line near Barrow-on-Soar, though there was never any through traffic. The descent ceases at the market town of Loughborough where the line renews its acquaintanceship with the Grand Union Canal, crossing it just north of the GC's station. Once again the line is on familiar embankments and bridges as it begins to climb northwards, crossing the Midland Main Line before striking out for another crossing of the river at Stanford-on-Soar. As it crosses the river, the line passes from Leicestershire into Nottinghamshire.

The maps are to the scale of 25ins to 1 mile, with north at the top, unless otherwise indicated.

HISTORICAL BACKGROUND

There has been a market at Rugby since the 13th Century. Its first railway was ... & Birmingham, which arrived in 1838.

From Rugby trains ran to Stafford from 1847, to Leicester via Wigston South from 1840 (to 1962), to Market Harborough from 1850 (to 1966), to Leamington from 1851 (to 1949) and to Northampton from 1881.

The Manchester, Sheffield and Lincolnshire Railway was formed in 1847 and was basically a northern enterprise, tapping the industrial heartlands of Yorkshire and the North Midlands. It had created links to the east and west coast ports on the Humber and Mersey, established hotels, canal and shipping interests, including becoming the first railway company to own seagoing ships in the mid 1860s. By the 1880s it was looking to head south.

This resulted in the building of the last main line to London and the first sod was cut on the 13th November 1894. To truly reflect the grandness of the scheme the directors of the MS&L applied for a change of name and on the 1st August 1897 the Great Central Railway Company was born. The route covered by this album opened to passengers on 15th March 1899, the line linking the northern end of the Metropolitan Railway with Nottingham.

On its way it passed over the 1862 railway from Nuneaton to Leicester and under the 1849 Swannington line. North of Loughborough, it crossed above the Midland Railway's main line.

The GCR became part of the London & North Eastern Railway in 1923. Upon nationalisation in 1948, the LNER became largely the Eastern Region of British Railways. The route was transferred to the London Midland Region on 1st February 1958 and closed to passengers on 5th September 1966 south of Rugby. Local trains continued north therof until 5th May 1969. Freight closure dates are given in the captions, as are those of intermediate stations.

Closure coincided with a rising tide of preservation fervour. Initially under the auspices of the Main Line Steam Trust, parts of the line between Loughborough and Leicester were earmarked for private operation. The gradual reopening of the line was southwards from Loughborough to Quorn, Rothley and the site of Belgrave & Birstall. The care of the new Great Central Railway has ensured that a small portion of the last main line to London can be enjoyed, recapturing somethng of its former glory over one hundred years later.

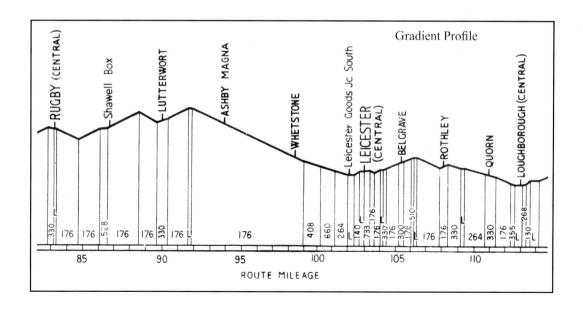

PASSENGER SERVICES

The route had three types of train: expresses between London and northern cities, notably Lilverpool, Manchester and Sheffield; expresses between the south coasts of England and Wales and a wide range of northern locations, plus local stopping trains. The middle group were particularly prolific on Summer Saturdays in the mid-1940s to the mid-1960s. Down services running on at least five days per week will be considered.

	Expresses		Local trains			
	Weekdays	Sundays	Weekdays		Sundays	
			A	B	A	B
1899	2	0	7	9	3	3
1911	3	0	7	16	5	5
1923	3	0	9	17	4	5
1944	6	5	5	7	0	3
1965	0	0	6	9	0	0
1969	0	0	0	6	0	0

A - South of Leicester B - North of Leicester

The expresses shown are only those which called at the terminal points of this album. They were reduced to a semi-fast service between Marylebone and Manchester on 4th April 1960.

January 1901

LONDON, AYLESBURY, BOURNEMOUTH, PORTSMOUTH, SOUTHAMPTON, OXFORD, RUGBY, LEICESTER, LOUGHBORO', NOTTINGHAM, SHEFFIELD, HUDDERSFIELD, HALIFAX, BRADFORD, LIVERPOOL, and MANCHESTER.—Great Central.

Down—Continued.	Week Days—*Continued from page 578.*														Sundays.											
	aft	aft	aft	aft	aft	aft	aft	aft	aft	aft	aft	aft	aft	mrn	mrn	mrn	mrn	aft	mrn	mrn	aft	aft	aft	aft	aft	aft
				1st and 3rd class Dining Car Express, London to Huddersfield, Halifax, and Bradford. / Through Corridor Carriage, London to Manchester.						Through Express, London to York.	Saturdays only.		London to Manchester Express. / Leaves Nottingham for Sheffield and beyond at 1 30 mrn.							Luncheon Car Express, London to Manchester.			Dining Car Express, London to Manchester.			
London (Marylebone) dep.				5 40				6 0		7 45			1020						9 30	11 0			5 0			7 0
Harrow-on-the-Hill								h		h			h						h				h			h
Pinner								h																		
Rickmansworth								h																		
Great Missenden								h																		
Aylesbury								h		h			h						h				h			b
Waddesdon **Manor**								h																		
Calvert								7 30											1047							8 17
Finmere, for Buckingham								7 42		9 2									1059							8 29
Brackley (Central) **360**	5 35							7 51		9 12									11 8				6 27			8 38
Helmdon	5 43							7 59											1116							8 46
Culworth	5 51							8 7											1124							8 54
86 Bournemouth (C.) dp																										
89 Portsmouth (Town) "			1240																							
86 Southamptn (Dks.) "			1 25																							
86 Winchester **28** "			2 8																							
Basingstoke **14** "			3 0																							
Reading **38** "			4 27																							
Didcot **38** "			3 28																							
Oxford (G.W.) dep.			5 22																							
Banbury "			6 10																							
Woodford and Hinton	5 58		6 30	7 10				8 14					12 2						1131							9 1
Charwelton	6 3							8 19											1136							9 6
Willoughby, for Daventry	6 15							8 31											1148							9 18
Rugby (Cn.) **346, 361, 359, [364**	6 24							8 40	9 5	9 45			1220				11 0		1157				6 58			9 27
Lutterworth	6 34							8 50	9 15	9 55							1110		12 7							9 37
Ashby Magna	6 42							8 58	9 23								1118		1215							9 45
Whetstone	6 51							9 7	9 32								1127		1224							9 54
Leicester (Cen.) **460, 504**	6 59	6 50		7 50			8 5	9 15	9 45	1017		1045	1252			8 0	1135		1240	1 14		2 0	7 25		7 40	10 2
Belgrave and Birstall	Stop	6 55					8 10		9 50			1050				8 5			1045			2 5			7 45	
Rothley		7 0					8 15	Stop	9 55			1055				8 10			1250			2 10			7 50	Stop
Quorn and Woodhouse		7 6					8 21		10 1			11 1				8 16			1256			2 16			7 56	
Loughboro' (Central) **360**		7 11					8 26		10 6	1032		11 6				8 21			1 1	1 29		2 21			8 1	
East Leake		7 20					8 35		1015			1115				8 30			1 10			2 30			8 10	
Ruddington		7 29					8 44		1024			1124				8 39			1 19			2 39			8 19	aft
Arkwright Street	aft	7 36					8 51	aft	1031			1131				8 46			1 26			2 46		8 0	8 26	9 20
Nottingham (Vic. Sta.)	7 10	7 41		8 22		8 33	8 56	9 40	1036	1054	1115	1136	1 21	1 25		8 51		1228	1 31	1 50	2 28	2 51	7 58	8 38	8 31	9 25
Carrington	7 13					8 36		9 43			1118					8 56		1231			2 31			8 41		9 28
New Basford	7 16	Stop				8 39		9 46			1121					8 59		1234			2 34	Stop		8 44		9 31
Bulwell Common	7 20					8 43		9 50			1125					9 3		1238			2 38			8 48		9 35
Hucknall Town	7 25					8 49		9 56			1130					9 9		1244			2 44			8 54		9 40
Kirkby and Pinxton						9 0		10 7							7 50	9 20		1255			2 55			9 5		
Tibshelf Town						9 10		1017							8 0	9 30		1 5			3 5			9 15		
Pilsley						9 13		1020							8 3	9 33		1 8			3 8			9 18		
Heath						9 18		1025							8 8	9 38		1 13			3 13			9 23		
Grassmoor		aft				9 24		1031							8 14	9 44		1 19			3 19	aft		9 29		
Chesterfield 459		7 35			8 50	9 31		1038							8 21	9 51		1 26			3 26	5 15		9 36		
Sheepbridge *		7 40			8 55	9 36		1043							8 26	9 56		1 31			3 31	5 20		9 41		
Staveley Works †		7 45			9 0	9 41		1048							8 31	10 1		1 36			3 36	5 25		9 46		
Staveley Town		7 49			9 4	9 45		1052							8 35	10 5		1 40			3 40	5 29		9 50		
Eckington and Renishaw		7 54			9 9	9 50		1057							8 40	1010		1 45			3 45	5 34		9 55		
Killamarsh		7 59			9 14	9 55		11 2							8 45	1015		1 50			3 50	5 39		10 0		
Beighton		8 4			9 19	10 0		11 7							8 50	1020		1 55			3 55	5 44		10 5		
Kiveton Park arr.				9c44	9 44	11c6									9 49							7 9				
Shireoaks "				9c49	9 49										9 54							7 14				
Worksop 574 "				9c54	9 54	1117	c								9 59							6c37				
Retford 295 "				10c9	1010	1130	c								1015							6c48				
	33	34	35	36	37	38	39	40	41	42	43	44	45	46	1	2	3	4	5	6	7	8	9	10	11	12

NOTES.

a Stop to take up on notice being given at the Station.

b Stops to set down from London on informing the Guard at London.

c *Via* Sheffield.

d Stop to set down on notice being given to the Guard at Sheffield.

e Change at Godley.

g Tuesdays and Saturdays.

h Stop to set down from London or take up for the Great Central Line.

i Except Sundays and Mondays.

k Saturdays only.

m Stops to set down from London on notice being given to the Guard at Nottingham.

n Passengers for Manchester (London Rd.) must change into the Slip Carriage at Sheffield.

Down. — Week Days—Continued.

(November 1930 timetable)

Station		
LONDON (Marylebone)	dep.	12 15 ... 3 20 ... 3 25 ... 4 55 5 0 ... 4 50 6 20 ... 6 27
High Wycombe	"	12 33 ... 3 57 ... 4 50 ... 5 39 ... 6 26 6 49
Princes Risboro	"	1 7 ... 5 8 ... 6 8 ... 6 49
Haddenham (Bucks)	"	... 6 18 ...
Wotton	"	...
Harrow-on-the-Hill **A**		... 6 26
Northwood	"	... 7 40
Aylesbury H 46, 442	"	... 4 13 4 45 5 24 ... 5 53 ... 7 5 7 49
Waddesdon	"	Stop 5 0 Stop ...
Quainton Road	"	... 6 24 ...
Calvert **C**	"	... 5 10 ... 6 38 7 28 7 35 ... 8 10
Finmere	"	1 38 ... 1 43 ... 5 17 ... 6 12 6 46 7 43 ... 8 19
Brackley **D** 466, 467	"	... 1 53 ... 5 27 ... 6 20 Stop 7 55 8 5 ... 8 27
Helmdon **F**, for Sulgrave	"	... 2 0 ... Stop 6 30 ... 7H42 8H40 Stop ... 8 39
Culworth	"	1 51 ...
Woodford & Hinton 727	arr.	3 7 ...
727 STRATFORD-ON-AVON	arr.	3 7 ...

Station (G.W.)		
98 BOURNEMOUTH CEN.	dep	11 6 ... 2 38 ... 2 32 ...
98 PORTSMOUTH **G**	"	11 0 ... 2 31 ...
98 SOUTHAMPTON TER.	"	12 p6 ...
47 BASINGSTOKE	"	1z18 ...
98 READING	"	1A54 ... 1 40 ... 1 10
17 PENZANCE	"	... 2 30 ... 2 0
17 PLYMOUTH **H**	"	8P40 ...
17 EXETER (St. David's)	"	10P0 ... 3X15
17 BRISTOL (Temple Md.)	"	12 0 ... 2 40
67 CARDIFF (General)	"	10 30 ... 6 20
17 SWINDON	"	1 30 ... 2 40
98 Oxford (G.W.)	dep.	2 35 ... 3 30 3 30 ... 7 5 7 42 ... 8 12
Banbury (Bridge St.)	"	12 55 ... 3F12 ... aft ... 8 34
727 Woodford & Hinton	arr.	1 20 ... 3 41 ... 6 35 ... 8 55
Woodford and Hinton	dep.	1 53 ... 2 13 3 33 ... 6 55 ... 9 1
Charwelton	"	... 2 18 ... 7 0 ... 9 5
Braunston and Willoughby	"	... 2 29 ... 7 9 ... 9 12
Rugby K 412, 468, 471	"	2 10 ... 2 38 3 51 ... 5 45 5 50 ... 7 21 ... 9 17 9 40
Lutterworth	'472	... 2 48 ... 6 3 8 0 ... 7 32 ... 9 47
Ashby Magna	"	... ... 6 8 ... 7 40 ... 9 51
Whetstone	"	... ... 6 12 ... 7 48 ... 10 1
Leicester (Central)	arr.	2 32 ... 3 13 4 13 5 9 5 11 5 18 6 20 6 25 6 43 7 17 7 56 8 14 8 37 ... 10 14
642,686, 688,690	dep.	2 36 ... 2 45 4 17 5 18 5 24 6 0 6 05 6 47 7 21 7 25 8 18 8 23 8 30 9 15 ... 10 45
Belgrave and Birstall	"	2 50 Stop 4 28 5 30 6 11 6 36 7 30 8 36 9 12 ... 10 51
Rothley	"	2 56 4 34 5 30 6 17 6 42 7 36 8 42 9 21 ... 10 57
Quorn and Woodhouse	"	3 2 4 40 5 36 6 22 7 48 8 46 9 32 ... 11 2
Loughboro (Cen.) L 642	"	2 50 3 7 4 30 4 45 5 41 6 30 7 35 7 56 Stop
East Leake	.687	3 15 4 50 5 52 6 23 7 59 9 42
Rushcliffe Halt	"	3 25 4 56 6 39 8 5 9 46
Ruddington	"	3 32 5 0 6 5 6 46 8 12 9 50
Arkwright Street	"	...
Nottingham (Victoria)	arr.	3 9 3 35 4 47 5 36 aft 6 49 7 12 7 54 8 15 8 41 8 50 9 13 9 59 ... 11 20
596, 899	dep.	3 9 3 15 3 20 4 25 4 51 4 58 5 38 5 48 6 13 6 15 Stop 7 30 7 14 Stop 8 0 8 37 8 45 8 50 9 13 ... 10 7 10 40
New Basford	"	3 23 3 25 4 30 ...
Bulwell Common	"	3 25 3 30 4 35 ... 8 10 ... 10 15
Hucknall (Cen.) **M**	"	3 31 3 36 4 41 6 6 6 34 7 41 8 16 8 58 9 4 ... 10 21 10 54
Kirkby-in-Ashfield (Cen.)	"	3 52 4 58 6 14 7 54 9 3 9 19 ... 11 9
Sutton-in-Ashfield (Cen.)	"	3 57 5 2 6 19 7 59 9 3 9 24 ... 11 14
Mansfield (L.N.E.) 903	arr.	4 7 5 9 6 25 8 5 9 20 9 30 ... 11 20

Marginal notes (November 1930): Restaurant Car, Marylebone to Manchester — Through Carriages from Bournemouth to Leeds (Central) — Restaurant Car, Marylebone to Halifax — Through Train, Leicester to Cleethorpes — Except Saturdays — Restaurant Car, Marylebone to Manchester (L.R.) — Via Aylesbury — Via High Wycombe — Through Carriage, Penzance to Swindon & Co. to York — Restaurant Car, Marylebone to Stratford-on-Avon and Banbury — Through Carriage, Marylebone to Aberdeen and Westbury to Glasgow, via Plymouth, Westbury — 1st and 3rd class Sleeping accommodation — Saturdays only — Except Weds. and Sats.

November 1930

LONDON (Marylebone), LEICESTER and NOTTINGHAM

Week Days

(February 1961 timetable)

Miles	Station		
—	London (Marylebone)	dep	1 35 ... 3 45 5 56 10 6k10 7 20 8 40 9N20 10 28 ... 12n22 12B40 12 34 ...
9¼	Harrow on the Hill		... 7 40 8 57 10 45 ... 1 21 12L13 12 49
27¼	High Wycombe		... 7 0 7 15 7k15 7L15 ... 10 50 10R50 ... 1 21 2 12L13 ...
36	Princes Risborough	A	... 7 20 7 33 7 50 8K27 ... 11 15 ... 2 10 12K40 ...
38½	Ilmer Halt		... 7 55 ... 2 15 ...
41½	Haddenham (Bucks)		... 7 30 7 43 8 1 ... 11 18 ... 2 21 ...
37½	Aylesbury (Town)		5X 9 ... 9 59 9 45 ... 12 2 ... 1B41 2 2 ...
44	Quainton Road		... Stop Stop 9 15 ... 12 11 Stop 2 12 ...
48½	Calvert		... 5U36 9 21 ... 12 19 ... 2 21 ...
54¼	Finmere		... 5U46 9 33 ... 12 28 ... 2 30 ...
59½	Brackley (Central)		... 9 44 10 10 ... 12 38 ... 2B 6 2 39 ...
62½	Helmdon		... 9 52 ... 12 46 ... 2 47 ...
69	Woodford Halse	arr	... 6 8 10 4 10 24 ... 12 58 ... 2 18 2 59 ...
—	217a Banbury General	dep	... ● Stop 9 35 ... 12J8 ... 3 15
71¾	Woodford Halse	dep	... 5 40 6 35 6 41 am 10 26 Stop 12 45 1 20 ...
71¾	Charwelton		... 6 41 am 10 32 12 51 ...
83¾	Rugby (Central)		... 3H43 6 5 7h 8 7 35 9 55 10 51 pm 2 10 2 41 3 55
90	Lutterworth		... 6 16 7 19 7 47 10 6 11 2 1 20 2 22 2 52 ...
93¾	Ashby Magna		... 6 23 7 27 7 55 10 14 1 28 2 30 ...
98½	Whetstone		... 6 33 7 36 8 4 10 23 1 37 2 39 ...
103	Leicester (Central)	arr	4 56 41 7 45 8 12 am 10 31 11 17 1 45 2 47 3 7 4 16
		dep	... 6 45 6 55 7 30 8 0 9 30 10 35 11 19 pm 1 0 3 11 4 22
105¼	Belgrave and Birstall		... 7 0 7 35 8 5 9 35 10 40 ... 1 5 ...
108	Rothley		... 7 6 8 11 9 41 10 46 ... 1 11 ...
110¾	Quorn and Woodhouse		... 6 57 7 12 7 44 8 17 9 47 10 52 ... 1 17 ...
113	Loughborough (Central)		... 7 2 7 18 7 49 8 23 9 52 10 58 11 33 1 22 3 25 4 36
117¼	East Leake		... 7 29 7 57 8 30 10 0 11 9 ... 1 30 ...
118¼	Rushcliffe Halt		... 7 10 7 32 8 34 10 6 11 16 ... 1 33 ...
122	Ruddington		... 7 39 8 41 10 10 ... 1 40 ...
123½	Arkwright Street		... 7 22 7 46 8 13 8 48 10 17 ... 1U45 ...
123½	Nottingham (Victoria)	arr	... 7 26 7 49 8 16 8 51 10 20 11 23 11 50 1 50 3 42 4 52
164½	Sheffield (Victoria)	arr	... 8 50 9 52 ... 7 0
177¼	Penistone	"	... 10 0 11 0 ... 7 20
201	Guide Bridge	"	... 10 29 11 31 ... 7 29
206	Manchester Piccadilly	"	... 10 40 11 41 ... 8d 5
212¼	(Central)	"	... 12 54 ... 7 54
241	Liverpool (Central)	"	... 12A15 12A15 ... 8 53
191	Huddersfield	"	... 10 35 12 48 ... 7 38
201½	Halifax (Town)	"	... 12T27 2z55 ... 9 4
203¾	Bradford (Exchange)	"	... 12 4 2 9 ... 8 20
211½	York	"	... 1P45 ... 7 42
219½	Newcastle	"	... 3P33 ... 10V11

Marginal notes (February 1961): Except Mondays — Saturdays only — Wednesdays and Saturdays — Saturdays only — TC Banbury Gen. to York (from 1st May), conveys RC and TC — Bournemouth West (dep 11 16 am) to York.

February 1961

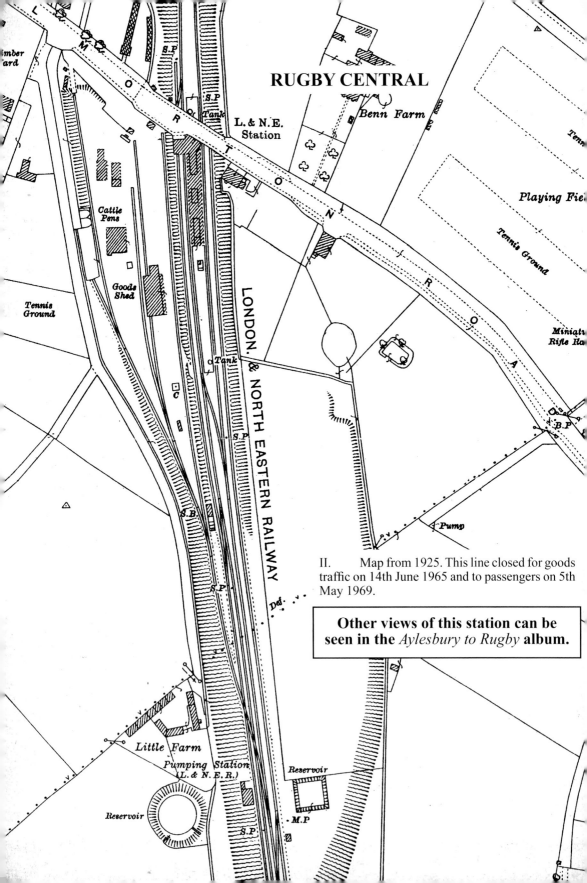

RUGBY CENTRAL

Benn Farm

L. & N.E. Station

Tank

S.P

S.P

Cattle Pens

Goods Shed

Tennis Ground

Tank

C

S.P

S.B.

S.P

S.P

LONDON. & NORTH EASTERN RAILWAY

Playing Fie

Tennis Ground

Miniatı Rifle Ra

B.P

Pump

Del

Little Farm

Pumping Station (L. & N.E.R.)

Reservoir

Reservoir

M.P

S.P

II.   Map from 1925. This line closed for goods traffic on 14th June 1965 and to passengers on 5th May 1969.

Other views of this station can be seen in the *Aylesbury to Rugby* album.

1.   A quiet moment on a sunny afternoon in 1952 shows the down platform looking north. Above the gents toilet on the right is the stationmaster's house overlooking the station and yard. Unusually this was not built by the railway company but already existed as Laurel Cottage prior to the arrival of the railway. The canopy, at 157 feet in length, protected buildings that contained various waiting rooms and the ladies toilet. The street level building as built had a chimney at each end of the roof but the one at the western end was subjected to two lightning strikes early in the Second World War resulting in it being dismantled. The down siding, in the foreground, extended into the goods yard headshunt making a total length of 640 yards. (L&GRP)

2.   The station was situated in the eastern suburbs of the town on Hillmorton Road. As we approach from the town centre this view looking south affords a glimpse of the goods facilities occupying 4 or 5 acres to the west of the main line. By the time this picture was taken around 1960 the goods depot building on the right had been taken over by Ross, a frozen food firm, as a distribution centre. In front of the building the local coal merchant continues to do business. The timber firm of Travis and Arnold also occupied the yard taking regular consignments of timber by rail until April 1964. Standing at the north end of the down siding is a set of coaches ready to be shunted to form a local service to Leicester or Nottingham. (D.C.Pearce coll.)

3.   An afternoon down express heads away, having called at the station, behind 'Britannia' 4-6-2 No. 70014 *Iron Duke* on 1st September 1962. Prominent in the background on the Hillmorton Road bridge is the station building. The fairly shallow banked cutting at this point is part of the longest on the line at one and three quarter miles in length. (D.C.Pearce coll.)

4.   Saturday 3rd September 1966 finds photographers and enthusiasts paying their last respects to the GC London Extension as a through route. Black 5 No. 45292 brings the 10.57 Nottingham Victoria to Neasden empty newspaper vans and ecs through. Across the platform, sister Black 5 No. 45267 waits in the down siding to shunt its coaches to form the last 12.30 local to Nottingham. The up loop, in the foreground, was created in 1941 to ease congestion but by now was largely redundant, through freight having been transferred away in June 1965. (E.Wilmshurst)

5.   At the north end of the down platform, and similarly at the south end of the up platform, watering facilities were provided for locomotives and here Black 5 No 44984 is refreshed en route to Nottingham with the 16.38 from Marylebone on 16th August 1966. Notice the cover over the top of the tank to prevent anything untoward ending up in the water. The length of bridge No.455 carrying Hillmorton Road over the railway is seen to advantage and the anxious activities of photographers indicates the anticipated closure of the line as a through route less than a month later on the 4th September. (R.J.Adderson)

6.   The station building on Hillmorton Road was something of a hotch-potch when viewed from the east. This is the up side showing the staircase down to the platform from a passageway alongside the main building. This passageway provided a separate exit from the station in addition to that in the main building. The sooty stain on the woodwork at the right hand end betrays the fact that the passageway straddled the up line. There was also a goods lift provided on this side of the station. The station had less than a month to go before final closure when this picture was taken on the 19th April 1969. (Gulliver coll.)

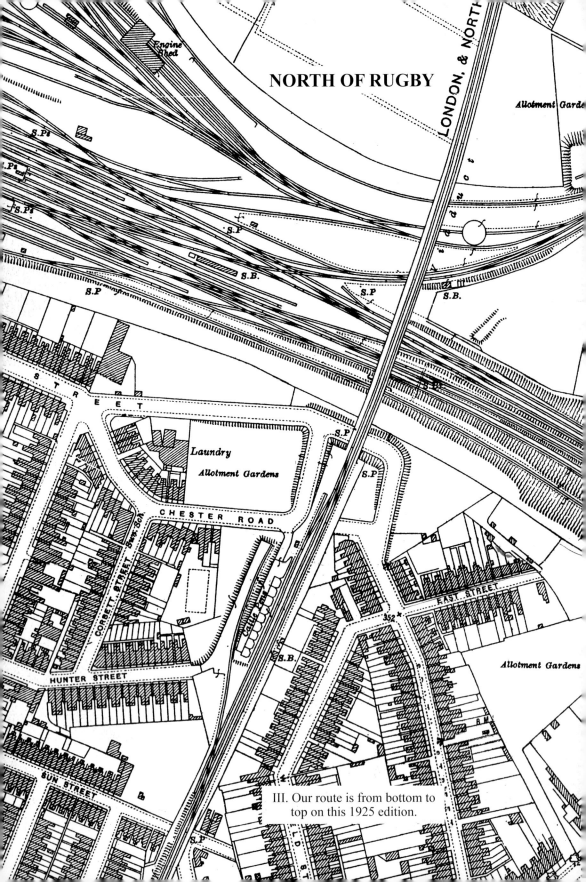

NORTH OF RUGBY

LONDON. & NORTH

Engine Shed

S.P.

S.P.

S.P.

S.P.

S.B.

S.P.

S.P.

S.B.

S.P.

Allotment Gardens

S.B.

STREET

Laundry

Allotment Gardens

S.P.

S.P.

CHESTER ROAD

CORBETT STREET

HUNTER STREET

EAST STREET

Allotment Gardens

S.B.

352

SUN STREET

S.P.

III. Our route is from bottom to top on this 1925 edition.

7.   Class B1 4-6-0 No 61093 brings the 15.02 Portsmouth Harbour to Sheffield train past the site of the signalbox and sidings serving the cattle market in August 1964. The box contained 30 levers to the standard GC Extension design and tended to be opened only on market days. It was closed in August 1953 and the sidings it controlled were dismantled. (D.Smith/Colour-Rail.com)

8.   Just north of the cattle sidings the GC crossed the LNW by the so-called 'bird-cage' bridge, or more prosaically bridge No 451, seen here in 1937 or 1938. We are looking in a north-westerly direction with the GC's line to Leicester disappearing off to the right across viaduct and embankment, elevating it across the Avon valley. The enormous signal gantry prominent in the centre of the picture was erected at the expense of the GC to compensate for sighting problems created when the bridge was constructed. It lasted until 1939 when it was dismantled as part of a local re-signalling scheme. Heading away for London is 'Jubilee' No. 5629 *Straits Settlements* as sister No. 5584 *North West Frontier* shunts empty stock. The final remains of the bridge itself were not dismantled until Christmas 2006. (Milepost 92½)

9.   We can now enjoy two pictures of Newton. As the line was being built, gravel was extracted from various locations to assist in its construction. One such location was here and when the line was completed a signal box was provided to control access to the main line. The view looking south from bridge 439 that carried Newton Lane over the railway shows the area where the siding was laid to the right in this view. The 20 lever signal box was located on the up side to the left of the train and, remarkably, only lasted for a couple of years before being moved to Aylestone near Leicester in 1901. The date is 6th May 1946 and the train is a V2 hauled Marylebone to Manchester express. (H.C.Casserley)

10.   We are now looking north towards the five arched bridge No 439 as an Annesley to Woodford freight hauled by 9F 2-10-0 No 92094 rattles south towards Rugby. The date is the 19th September 1964 and the brick recess in the cutting side to the right of the loco accommodated the signal box. (J.S.Gilks)

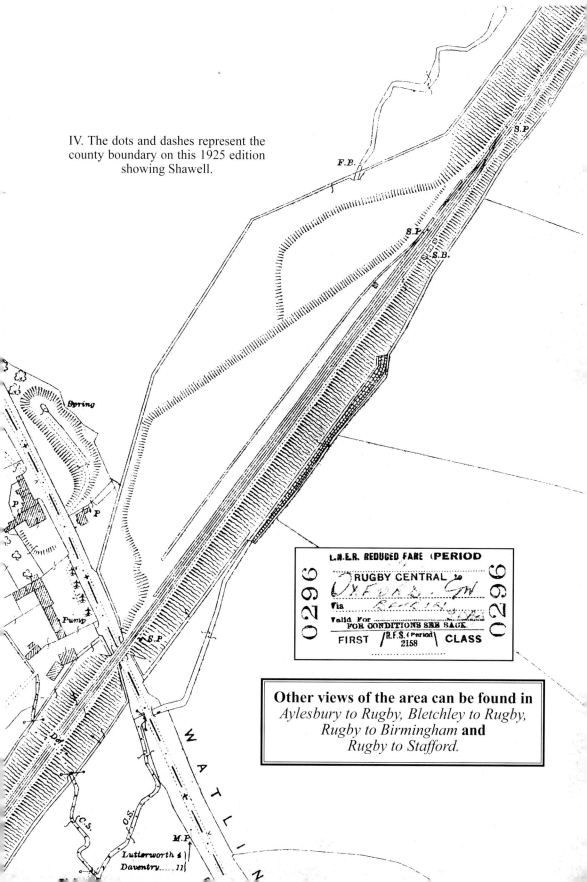

IV. The dots and dashes represent the county boundary on this 1925 edition showing Shawell.

F.B.

S.P.

S.P.

S.B.

Spring

P

P

Pump

S.P.

L.N.E.R. REDUCED FARE (PERIOD

0296   0296

RUGBY CENTRAL to
OXFORD GW
Via BRACKLEY
Valid for
FOR CONDITIONS SEE BACK
FIRST   R.F.S. (Period) 2158   CLASS

Other views of the area can be found in
Aylesbury to Rugby, Bletchley to Rugby,
Rugby to Birmingham **and**
Rugby to Stafford.

W A T L I N

C.S.

O.S.

M.P.

Lutterworth 4
Daventry 11

11.   Just to the north of the point where the line crossed Watling Street it had been planned to build a station but only a signal box and siding were eventually constructed. The signal box shown here was built on the up side as witnessed by this southbound freight hauled by another 9F. The view was taken on the 2nd January 1965 and shows the down intermediate block signal that replaced the 20 lever box on closure on the 10th May 1959. An arson attack shortly afterwards reduced the building to the burnt out shell seen here. (M.Mitchell)

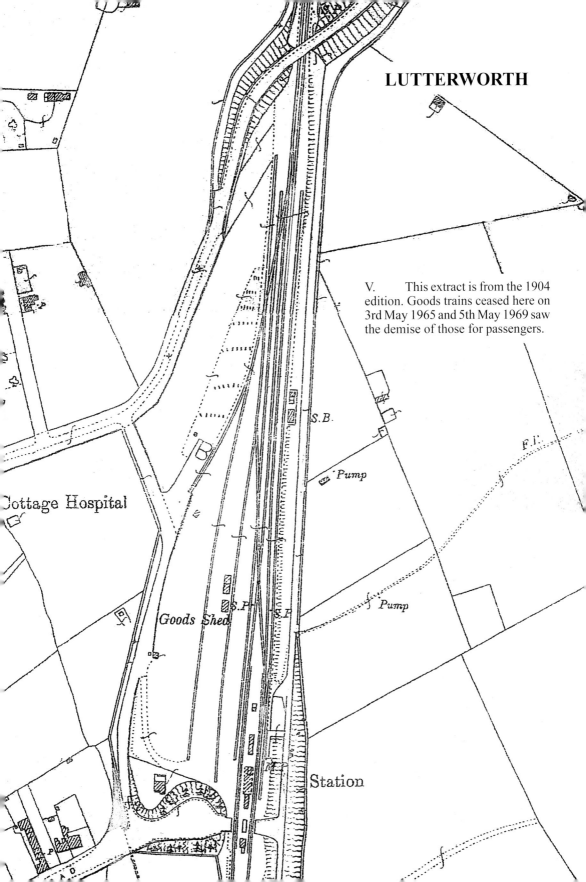

LUTTERWORTH

V.   This extract is from the 1904 edition. Goods trains ceased here on 3rd May 1965 and 5th May 1969 saw the demise of those for passengers.

S.B.

Pump

F.P.

Cottage Hospital

Pump

Goods Shed *S.P.* *S.P.*

Station

12.   We are 90 miles from London and, in 1938, Lutterworth had a population of 2395, which remained more or less the same until the line closed just over thirty years later. It was only after closure that it began to increase to its present size of nearly 8300. The station was another example of the standard pattern of platform design for the line with an island platform, though this time accessed from the street below in Station Road. This turn of the century view is from the town looking east towards the station with the station masters house on the left and the station itself in the background. (P.Laming coll.)

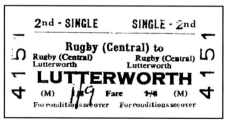

13.   A closer view of the down platform, taken on the 15th August 1955, looking north reveals the covered entrance from the street and the combined seat and running in board common to all of the smaller stations on the extension. The canopy protects the circulating area next to the small booking office and the building beyond contained the waiting room and ladies toilet – the gents making do with the building towards the far end of the platform. In later years the space between these two buildings was occupied by a small cycle shed. In the distance, situated on the up side, was the 40 lever signal box which closed on the 20th June 1965. (Milepost 92½)

14.   We are standing on the up platform near the top of the stairs from Station Road in the summer of 1955. The view is looking north towards the signal box and, although not sharp, shows the trailing crossover from the up refuge siding and the small cattle dock, together with a milepost proclaiming 116 miles. Despite the fact that we are 90 miles from London the milepost refers to the mileage from Manchester, ironically betraying the 'branch' nature of the London Extension from the established routes of the company to the north! (Milepost 92½)

15.   The date is the 19th July 1959 and V2 2-6-2 No. 60831 hauls a Sheffield to Swindon train. The building to the left of the train contains the porters room, separated from the main station buildings by the bridge over the road from the town. Notice how the bridge abutments over Station Road have been constructed to make allowance for the possibility of an additional running line, an aspiration that never materialised. The tall chimney in the right background belonged to the Wycliffe Iron Foundry. (J.S.Gilks)

16.   A general track level view looking south shows the down platform with the boarded crossing linking the platform with the goods yard on the right across the down refuge siding in the foreground. This had room for the standage of 61 wagons plus an engine and brake van. Unlike several of the other stations, this one was not provided with loops in either direction to pass trains. This picture was taken on 12th May 1962. (R.M.Casserley)

17.   Looking south from near the signal box in 1965 a clearer view is afforded of the gents toilets together with the running in board at the other end of the platform. By now a maroon enamel board announces the location confirming that the line is now under the auspices of the London Midland Region. In the foreground the truncated remains of the siding to the cattle dock can be seen as a spur off the up refuge siding, itself able to accommodate an engine, brake van and 65 wagons. (Lens of Sutton)

NORTH OF LUTTERWORTH

18.   Just to the north of the station an iron foundry was established in 1906 under the auspices of the Wycliffe Foundry Company Ltd and a private siding was provided for 11 wagons, an arrangement that remained right through until the late 1950s. This view, taken from the Gilmorton Road bridge looking north on the 7th May 1966, shows Black 5 No. 45288 approaching with the 17.30 Nottingham Victoria to Rugby passing the foundry, its siding and the site of the wharf. Access was provided via a trailing connection controlled by a 2 lever ground frame electrically released from the signal box. By now the box had been closed for eleven months, hence the signal post (the former up home signal) bereft of its arm to the right of the train. (D.C.Pearce coll.)

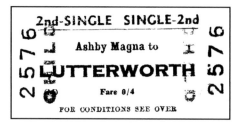

SOUTH OF ASHBY MAGNA

19.   Just south of the station at Ashby Magna a tunnel (No 414) was constructed, 92 yards in length, which carried a minor road between Dunston Bassett and Gilmorton over the railway. In this view, looking north, Stanier 2-6-4T No. 42453 emerges with the 12.35 (SO) Leicester to Rugby local on the 8th July 1961. (M.Mitchell)

20.   We are now on top of the tunnel looking north on the 26th October 1963 as the 12.30 Nottingham to Marylebone DMU gets away from Ashby Magna, seen in the middle distance, at 1.17pm. On a line characterised by its embankments and cuttings this picture gives some idea of the immense earthworks involved in its construction. The infant M1 is on the right, sounding the final death knell for the line. (J.S.Gilks)

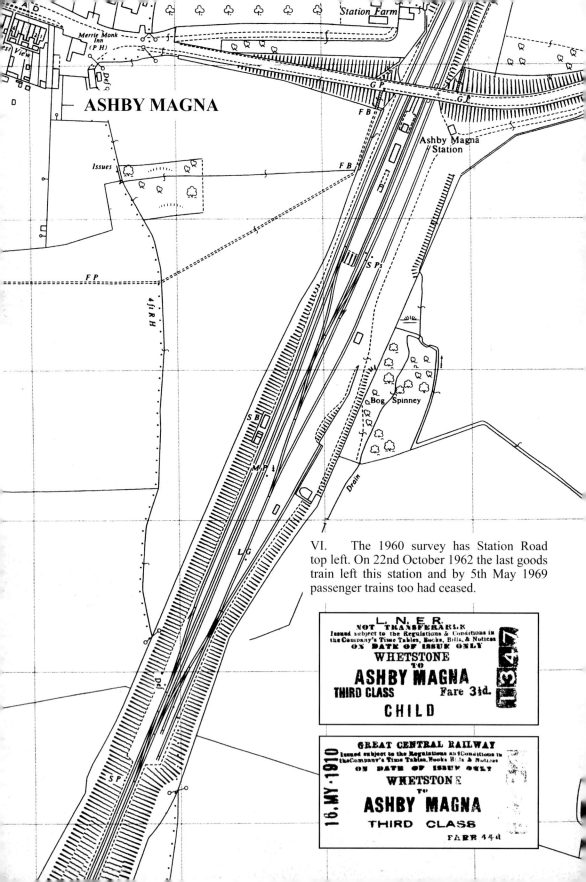

ASHBY MAGNA

Merrie Monk
Inn
(P H)

Station Farm

Ashby Magna
Station

FB

Issues

FB

S Ps

FP

4 ft R H

Bog Spinney

S B

M P

Drain

L G

SP

Def

VI.   The 1960 survey has Station Road
top left. On 22nd October 1962 the last goods
train left this station and by 5th May 1969
passenger trains too had ceased.

L. N. E. R.
NOT TRANSFERABLE
Issued subject to the Regulations & Conditions in
the Company's Time Tables, Books, Bills, & Notices
ON DATE OF ISSUE ONLY
WHETSTONE
TO
ASHBY MAGNA
THIRD CLASS   Fare 3½d.
CHILD

1347

GREAT CENTRAL RAILWAY
Issued subject to the Regulations and Conditions in
the Company's Time Tables, Books Bills & Notices
ON DATE OF ISSUE ONLY
WHETSTONE
TO
ASHBY MAGNA
THIRD CLASS
FARE 4½d.

16. MY. 1910

21.	This rather delightful rustic view looking east was taken in the 1920s from just outside the "Railway Hotel" on the road from Dunston Bassett to Ashby Magna, seen on top of the hill a half mile distant beyond the railway. St Mary's church is prominent together with the station masters house to the left of the bridge. The house disappeared with the building of the M1 motorway. (P.Laming coll.)

22.	Typical of the smaller stations on the line, a simple entrance and stairs gave access to the island platform, this time playing host to the 17.30 Nottingham to Rugby local hauled by L1 2-6-4T no. 67758 as it calls on this very pleasant evening in 1960. We are on the west side of the line overlooking the down passenger loop and down main alongside the platform. Beyond the train is the small goods yard overlooked by the station masters house to the right. The tall repeater signal in the middle of the picture, operated by lever No 8 in the signal box, was designed for sighting purposes to give a clear view to enginemen in charge of up trains that would otherwise be obscured by the overbridge. (M.Mitchell)

23.   The signal box contained 40 levers and in 1961, when this picture was taken, was open continuously. Nestling in the cutting this side of the box is the lamp hut where the lamps for the signals were tended and prepared. Leicester based class V2 2-6-2 No 60890 passes with the 10.19 York to Bournemouth West, made up of Southern Region stock. In a typical 24 hour period on a weekday in 1955 an average of 58 up train and 57 down train movements would be recorded in the register, though fascinatingly, during the ASLEF strike from the end of May until the 15th June that year only 5 in each direction would be recorded. This despite the box remaining open continuously! The box finally closed with the cessation of through services on the 4th September 1966. (M.Mitchell)

24.   It is FA Cup Final day, 6th May 1961, and Leicester are up for the honours at Wembley. Immaculate Black 5 4-6-0 No 45267 roars through with a supporters' special as a V2 heads north with a Woodford to York fitted freight. This beautifully timed picture provides a glimpse of the diminutive goods yard with its depot building on the left. A small coal yard was provided together with a cattle dock just beyond the building, all closed on the 22nd October 1962. (M.Mitchell)

25.   In this view, taken on the 12th May 1962, we are looking towards Leicester with the bridge spanning the down lines to the same design as that spanning the up lines. It also shows the entrance to the gents and the flowerbed designed to soften the features of the running in board and generally the pride and joy of the station staff. Just beyond and to the right can be glimpsed the weighbridge at the entrance to the goods yard. (R.M.Casserley)

26.   At the bottom of the stairs down from the road the standard arrangement of buildings is revealed in this view showing the southbound platform in 1965. Curiously, the canopy on all the minor stations only extended over the ticket office – access to the waiting rooms, ladies, bike shed and gents was exposed to the elements. (Lens of Sutton)

27.   The view from the south end of the station looking north in 1965 shows the concentration of buildings on the island platform together with the running in board announcing the location. A good view is also afforded of the bridge spanning the up lines, the nearest being the up passenger loop with the up main serving the platform. The up and down passenger loops were wartime additions constructed in 1941 to ease congestion on what, at the time, was a very busy line. (Lens of Sutton)

28.   Class 9F 2-10-0 No 92032 approaching from the north with an empty oil tank train from Abbey Lane Sidings for Fawley on the evening of 11th June 1965; this was the last scheduled through freight working on the GC. As Woodford shed also closed from the same date, Banbury shed became responsible for providing power for GC line services - pretty clear what the ultimate intention was! The M1 motorway is seen to the right of the photograph. (D.Bodicoat)

SOUTH OF WHETSTONE

29.   An interesting view taken on 25 February 1963 at Cosby shows "Royal Scot" 4-6-0 No 46111 *Royal Fusilier* with a down semi-fast passing slowly over the beginnings of the bridge which was to be built across the M1 motorway. It can be seen that the bridge has been fabricated and is almost ready to be rolled into place. The photographer was standing, if not on, where the M1's hard shoulder would be, certainly within an area where few would wish to stand nowadays! (D.Bodicoat)

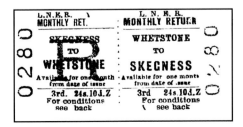

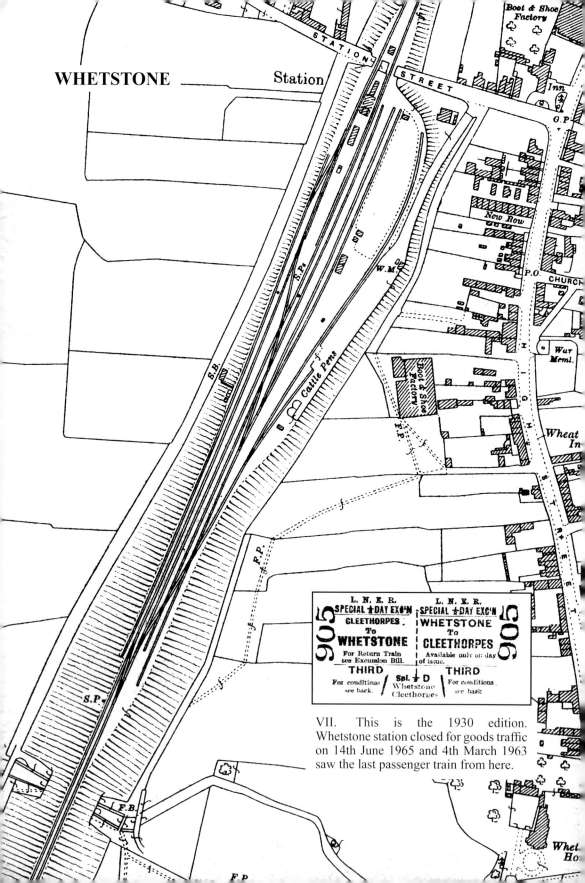

WHETSTONE — Station

Boot & Shoe Factory

Inn

STATION STREET

New Row

P.O. CHURCH

War Meml.

Wheat In

Boot & Shoe Factory

Cattle Pens

S.B.

W.M.

S.P.

S.P.

F.B.

F.P.

L.N.E.R.	L.N.E.R.
SPECIAL ½ DAY EXC'N	SPECIAL ½ DAY EXC'N
CLEETHORPES	WHETSTONE
To	To
WHETSTONE	**CLEETHORPES**
For Return Train see Excursion Bill.	Available only on day of issue.
THIRD	**THIRD**
For conditions see back.	For conditions see back.

905 / Spl. ½ D Whetstone Cleethorpes / 905

VII. This is the 1930 edition. Whetstone station closed for goods traffic on 14th June 1965 and 4th March 1963 saw the last passenger train from here.

30.　　Similar in design to Lutterworth, the platform was accessed via steps up from the road below. Up on the platform in the late 1940s the view north towards Leicester shows the main running in board and the characteristic arrangement of the station buildings. Trailing into the down main on the left is the down refuge siding and beyond is the bridge over Station Street, again, as at Lutterworth, showing the abutments prepared for an unrealised aspiration. (Stations UK)

31.　　The view north towards Leicester from the signal box on the pleasant morning of the 7th June 1959 finds a class 9F making steady progress south with a train of fitted vans from York for the Western Region. In the foreground is the down refuge siding, which could take 51 wagons plus an engine and brake van. Glimpsed in the goods yard to the right of the train is the small goods depot building, soon to be dwarfed by the cement depot established in 1963. (Milepost 92½)

32.   Black 5 No 44665 passes with the 1.58 p.m. train from Leicester to Marylebone on 24 Feb 1963, the penultimate Sunday on which day time trains ran on the line on Sundays. To the right of the train cement silos can be seen under construction in the goods yard. There was still plenty of snow and ice around at the end of that unforgettable winter, as can be seen on the bridleway on the left. (D.Bodicoat)

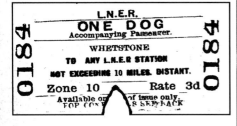

33.   This view, taken in 1964 from the bridleway, shows 'Britannia' 4-6-2 No 70020 *Mercury* with an afternoon semi-fast from Marylebone to Nottingham passing the signal box and lamp hut. The 40 lever box closed on the 5th September 1965. (MLPG)

→ 34. The view from the top of one of the cement silos looking south in the summer of 1964 shows some of the Presflo wagons that were used for the cement traffic. It also gives a different perspective on the all wooden signal box and lamp hut together with a freshly ballasted down line. Across the top of the picture, from left to right, can be glimpsed the M1 motorway extension that was nearing completion. (F.Allen/D.Bodicoat coll.)

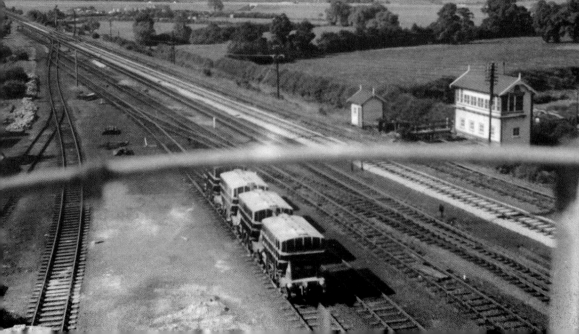

35.   This was the only station between Leicester and Rugby to lose its passenger services, before the route closure in 1969, having closed on the 4th March 1963. In this 1964 view we are looking along the up platform towards Rugby. Despite this, the clock is still functioning above the booking office window. On the left are more Presflo wagons serving the Rugby Cement sidings in the goods yard. With the wholesale withdrawal of freight services from the line in 1965, it is believed the depot was transferred to Syston on the neighbouring Midland main line. (Lens of Sutton)

36.   As we look towards Leicester on a glorious summer morning in 1964 the closed station is over to the left and in the left foreground there is the former Aylestone signalbox, which was in the yard at Whetstone for almost as long as anyone could remember. This was its third resting place having been at Newton, then at Aylestone before it was closed in 1925 and it seems likely it was transported the two miles here shortly afterwards. Also to be seen is the coal merchants' stacking areas, moved to that location from the space that was taken up by the cement silos when they were erected early in 1963. (F.Allen/D.Bodicoat coll.)

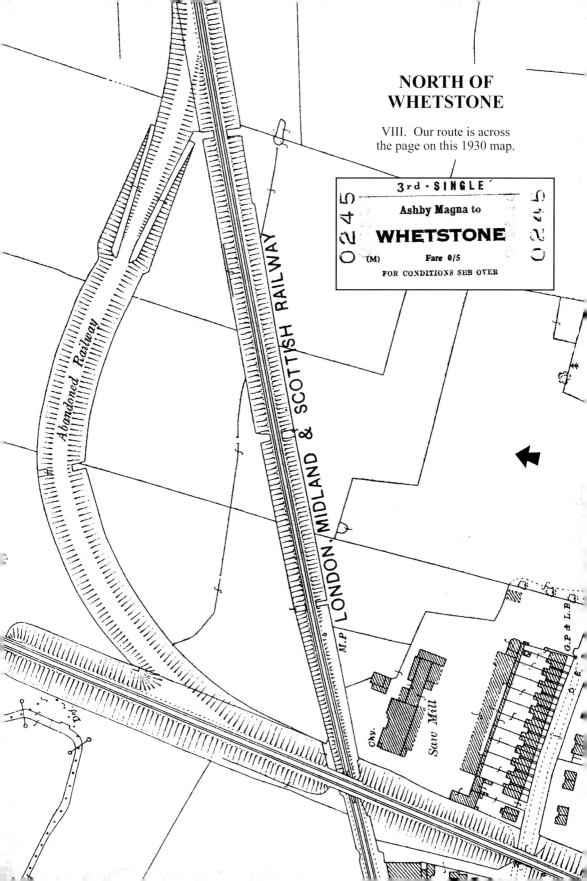

NORTH OF WHETSTONE

VIII. Our route is across the page on this 1930 map.

3rd · SINGLE

Ashby Magna to

WHETSTONE

(M)   Fare 0/5

FOR CONDITIONS SEE OVER

0245   0245

Abandoned Railway

LONDON, MIDLAND & SCOTTISH RAILWAY

M.P

Saw Mill

Cwy.

G.P & L.B

37.   To the north of the station the GC crossed the LNW Leicester to Nuneaton line by the bridge (No 396) seen in the foreground in this view looking north towards Leicester on the 11th August 2010. There was once a link between the two lines constructed to assist the building of the Extension before being disconnected on completion. The line was reinstated during the First World War and branched off to the right just beyond the end of the bridge seen here. It was closed permanently in 1919. The junction was controlled by a 14 lever signal box which was situated on the left beyond the bridge parapet, linked to Blaby Junction on the Nuneaton line. For many years, the earthworks of this link could be seen on the eastern side of the line to the right of this view. (D.C.Pearce)

38.   The line now strikes out across the valley of the River Sence, itself a tributary of the River Soar, by embankment and Whetstone Viaduct. It crosses the river by a 13 arch viaduct (No 395), seen here on the 11th August 2010. The blue bricks that form the arches are so redolent of the bridge builder's art and characterised the many bridges, abutments and tunnels that featured on the line. (D.C.Pearce)

39.   A point 1 mile 1188 yards north of Whetstone Junction was where the former Newton signal box was moved to in 1901. It was appropriately renamed Aylestone and was 1 mile 1254 yards south of Leicester Goods South signal box. It was situated on the down side and closed by September of 1924 as a result of local signalling alterations in connection with the introduction of intermediate block signals between Whetstone and Leicester. Inexplicably, working timetables for the following five or six years until about 1930 made reference to its closure, but indicated it to be 56 yards nearer Leicester! This view of the 20 lever box around 1912 shows the signalman. (A.West coll.)

SOUTH OF LEICESTER

Goods South

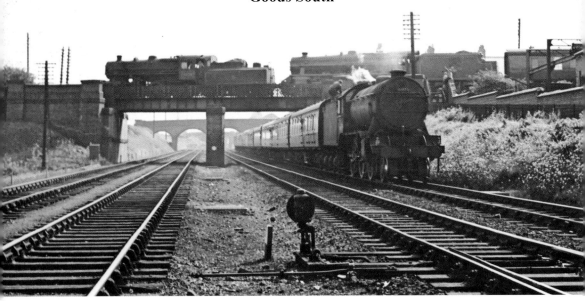

40.   Class K3 No 61975 has brought the Bournemouth - Newcastle to a stand under the Midland Railway's Leicester to Burton branch. Coming in from the Burton direction is the Saturdays only Blackpool to Leicester, hauled by an unidentified Ivatt 2-6-0 and a Stanier Black 5 4-6-0. We are looking towards Whetstone in this 1958 view and the lines from left to right are the goods yard headshunt, the down goods arrival line, the up main and the down main. (Milepost 92½)

41.   Looking in the other direction from near the Burton line bridge, this 1963 view shows the Newcastle - Bournemouth hauled by one of Sheffield Darnall's English Electric type 3s that had taken over these workings. The terraced houses in Western Road are very evident on the left as the line threads the southern suburbs of Leicester. (D.C.Pearce coll.)

42. The view from the other side of the line, looking north, shows the sidings adjacent to the loco depot, which is off to the right. BR Standard Class 5 No 73159 is heading south with the 17.15 Nottingham to Marylebone on this glorious evening in 1964. The path along the back of the houses on Western Road on the left was a favourite haunt of enthusiasts and observers of GC traffic. (M.Mitchell)

43. The 60 lever signal box contained much to occupy a busy signalman. Not only did it control traffic on the main line but also movements to and from the loco shed, which was on the extreme left in this view looking south. It also oversaw movements on the goods lines as well as access to Braunstone Gate goods yard. Small wonder, until the cessation of the majority of goods traffic and its closure on the 13th June 1965, the box was normally booked to remain open continuously. The picture offers a glimpse of the line that was constructed in 1965 to link the goods yard with the Burton line, just to the left of the signal box. It saw regular use until December 1995. The goods lines in the foreground lie thick with rust and the bracket signal minus its arms are testimony to the final decline that had set in when pictured in 1966. (C.Weightman/A.Bullimore coll.)

44.   This general view taken in the mid-1950s from behind the Goods South signal box looking roughly south-eastwards shows local class J11 No. 64375 on the "coal stage shunt". To the left can be seen the shed building and locomotive yard. The class J11 is re-arranging empty and loaded coal wagons for the elevated coal stage that is just behind the locomotive. Over to the right lies the former coal stacking ground and additional goods sidings. Beyond is the Leicester to Burton line bounding the south side of the site. (Milepost 92½)

45.   The bracket signal controlling access to the loco depot, yard and headshunt, together with the exit onto the up main from the up goods line, is prominent in this view of the goods yard pilot, standing near the shunter's cabin just out of view to the left. class J52 No 68839 was the resident pilot from 1952 until its withdrawal in 1958 when it was replaced by an LMS 'Jinty'. The line it is standing on was a shunting road between the main goods yard at Braunstone Gate and the loco yard, ironically becoming the remaining link to the Burton line, seen crossing in the distance beyond the signal box, when the main line closed. (Milepost 92½)

46.   The next bridge (No 378) to the north carried Upperton Road over the railway and also straddled the entrance to Braunstone Gate goods yard. The main and goods lines occupied the space in the foreground by now converted to a footpath in this view from the 16th February 1988. Redundant coaches awaiting scrapping stand by the entrance to Braunstone Gate, marked by the plated section of the bridge, and, on the right, the building housing the former wagon repair shops is prominent, no longer railway owned. No 20048 brings some loaded wagons out of Frank Berry's scrapyard. The Upperton Road viaduct was dismantled in 2007. (D.C.Pearce)

47.   We are now looking south from Upperton Road bridge with the houses on Western Road on the right. This view dates from 19th April 1969 and shows the up and down main on the right, the up and down goods lines in the middle and the entrance to Braunstone Gate goods yard on the left. The Forester Railtour was run by the RCTS and is making its way along the up goods line before taking the chord up onto the Burton line behind the signal box in the distance. (Courtney-Haydon coll./RCTS)

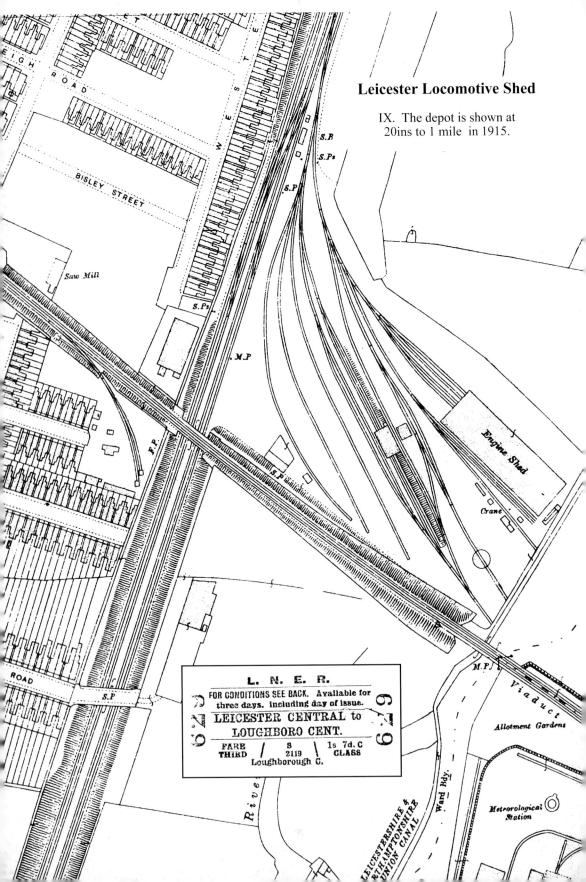

Leicester Locomotive Shed

IX. The depot is shown at
20ins to 1 mile in 1915.

BISLEY STREET

Saw Mill

S.B
S.Ps
S.P.

S.Ps

M.P

F.P.

S.P

Engine Shed

Crane

M.P.

Viaduct

Allotment Gardens

ROAD

S.P

L. N. E. R.
FOR CONDITIONS SEE BACK. Available for
three days. Including day of issue.
LEICESTER CENTRAL to
LOUGHBORO CENT.
FARE | S | 1s 7d. C
THIRD | 2119 | CLASS
Loughborough C.

River

Ward Bdy.

Metorological
Station

LEICESTERSHIRE &
NORTHAMPTONSHIRE
UNION CANAL

48.   This general view of the small shed from the mid-1930s suggests something of its status as an important staging point for engine change on the main line. The four road shed could accommodate up to 20 engines and was typical of the style of building for the sheds provided for the London Extension. To the right, the building with the chimney was provided to dry sand and next to it the coaling stage. (D.C.Pearce coll.)

49.   This view shows the sand dryer on the left and the coaling stage in 1957. The embankment leading to the stage itself was to gain the necessary height and ease the transfer of coal between wagon and loco. Local V2 No 60879 completes the scene. The water tank above the coaling stage had a capacity for 75,000 gallons. (Midland Railway Trust)

50.   Alongside the offices, stores and workshops there were further storage roads including one that served the shear legs. In attendance in this mid 1950s view can be seen various locos laying over including two J11 0-6-0s Nos 64375 and 64330, flanking A3 No 60102 *Sir Frederick Banbury* at home and another locomotive whose identity has eluded the camera. Just out of view to the right was the 55ft 1ins turntable in an exposed spot between the shed and the Leicester to Burton line embankment. The prominent chimney served the smithy. (Milepost 92½)

51.   A lovely evening in 1957 finds class 04 No. 63624 from Sheffield Darnall shed keeping company with locally based class A3 No 60111 *Enterprise* on the two centre roads of the shed. The class A3 is being prepared to take the "Master Cutler" onwards from Leicester to Sheffield later that evening. Overlooking the shed yard and dominating the scene to the left are the chimneys of Leicester's power station just the other side of the River Soar/Grand Union Canal, the tow path of which runs along the back of the shed and provided many a spotter unofficial access to the yard. (Milepost 92½)

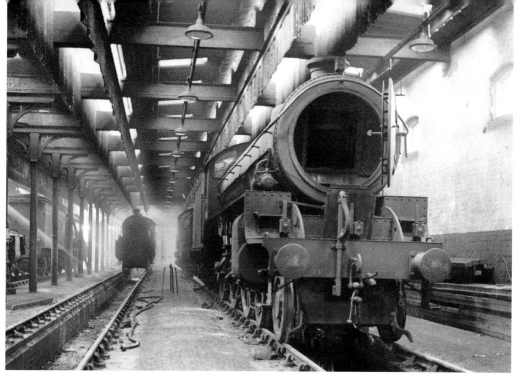

52.		By the early 1950s the original north-light roof of the shed was becoming badly in need of repair following the ravages of time, the mixture of heat and soot from the chimneys of countless locos, not to mention a war where maintenance of infrastructure was as scarce as that for rolling stock. The roof was duly replaced and this 1957 view shows the gentle pitch of the new roof over each shed road, together with the more modern lighting that was installed at the same time. The class B1 on the right is undergoing some routine maintenance and beyond a couple of sisters, together with a class A3, rest in the cool of the interior. The shed closed on 6th July 1964. (Milepost 92½)

53.		The view from the power station roof in 1967 provides a glimpse of the derelict yard and associated buildings. The shed retains its northlight roof over the offices, workshops and stores compared to the new roof over the running shed. The protruding section of roof was above the internal lifting gear on the road nearest the workshop and smithy, the chimney of which can be seen just beyond. Just to the left of the pylons, is the coal stage and crumbling sand house. The link to Braunstone Gate goods yard from the Burton line swings down behind the coal stage from left to right and was opened in 1965 to provide access for trip working to and from the yard as well as Abbey Lane in the absence of the through freight killed off at the time. (N.Tout)

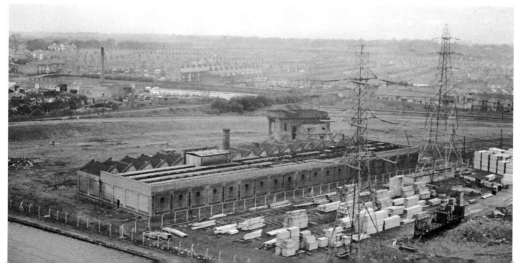

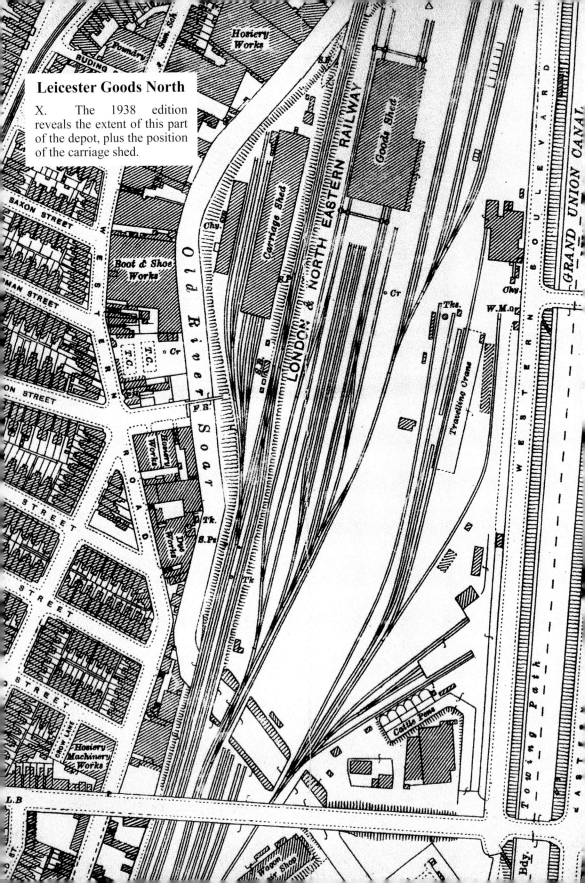

Leicester Goods North

X. The 1938 edition reveals the extent of this part of the depot, plus the position of the carriage shed.

54.   This general view looking north from Upperton Road shows the four-road carriage shed to the left of the main lines in the left foreground. The date is the 19th April 1969 and the RCTS' 200th railtour, the 'Forester' from Coventry, is making its way along the up goods line. Beyond is Braunstone Gate goods yard, by now reduced to handling mainly coal, trip worked from the Midland via the Burton line chord. (Courtney-Haydon coll./RCTS)

55.   Looking across from the signal box in the mid 1950s it can be seen that the sidings full of wagons in Braunstone Gate goods yard are at a slightly lower level. The main running lines are rising up to meet the end of the viaduct that leads to Central station. Also to be seen are the roofs of some coaches, as the yard invariably was used to stable the odd rake of passenger stock. The two light engines, the leading one of which is class J11 No. 64364, are on the down goods line awaiting separate paths to the station from the shed. In the foreground are the up and down main and, to the left of the class J11, the up goods line. (Milepost 92½)

56.   The 40-lever Goods North signal box controlled access to the north end of the goods lines as well as the carriage sidings to the west of the mainline. The trailing connection to them can be seen leading away behind the box on the right. This late 1960s view looking south also shows Upperton Road viaduct together with the tall down home signal with its twin signal arms. It also carried distant signals for Leicester Passenger South box. Remarkably throughout its life, over half the levers in this box were spare and it closed on 4th May 1969.
(C.Weightman/A.Bullimore coll.)

57.   On the 23rd December 1986 the view north from Upperton Road bridge offers a glimpse of the Old River Soar as it meanders its way through the city to the left of the footpath. Braunstone Gate goods yard, by now occupied by the scrapyard of Vic Berry, is to the right of the footpath, appropriately called Great Central Way. Brother Frank also owned a scrapyard alongside. The goods warehouse is prominent on the skyline in the middle distance beyond the stacked coach bodies and, to the right, in front of the church spires, the building with the tower was the electricity and hydraulic power house. Much use was made of hydraulics in the goods yard, particularly for powering capstans to assist in moving wagons in and around the yard. (D.C.Pearce)

58.   On the west side between the main running lines and the river a wooden four-road carriage cleaning shed was provided together with a gas works and three additional sidings. These were rendered largely redundant with the cessation of local services from Leicester and the closure of the line as a through route. This early 1970s view shows the floor of the former sheds together with the old gas works and stables on the left, the river is out of sight, just beyond. (N.Tout)

59.　　The bow string bridge carrying the railway over Braunstone Gate, seen here looking east in the 1990s, became something of a 'cause celebre' when it was threatened with demolition. The skew span dictated by the site meant that the lattice girders were of unequal length. A vigorous public campaign to save the bridge was begun by the *Leicester Mercury* in 1996 and lasted for thirteen years. It was dismantled in November 2009. The view illustrates the flamboyant way in which the railway was boldly carried across the west side of the city with several examples of this style of bridge building incorporated into the overall length of the viaduct. (M.J.Clarke)

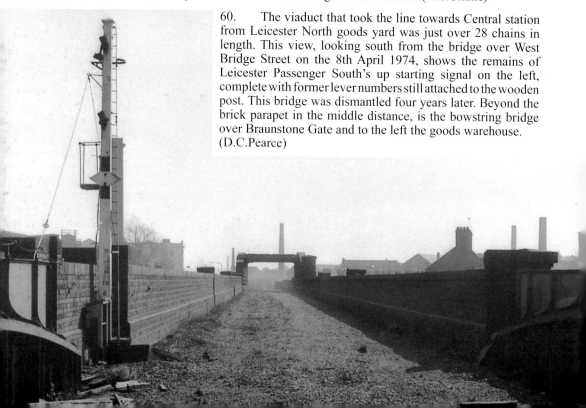

60.　　The viaduct that took the line towards Central station from Leicester North goods yard was just over 28 chains in length. This view, looking south from the bridge over West Bridge Street on the 8th April 1974, shows the remains of Leicester Passenger South's up starting signal on the left, complete with former lever numbers still attached to the wooden post. This bridge was dismantled four years later. Beyond the brick parapet in the middle distance, is the bowstring bridge over Braunstone Gate and to the left the goods warehouse. (D.C.Pearce)

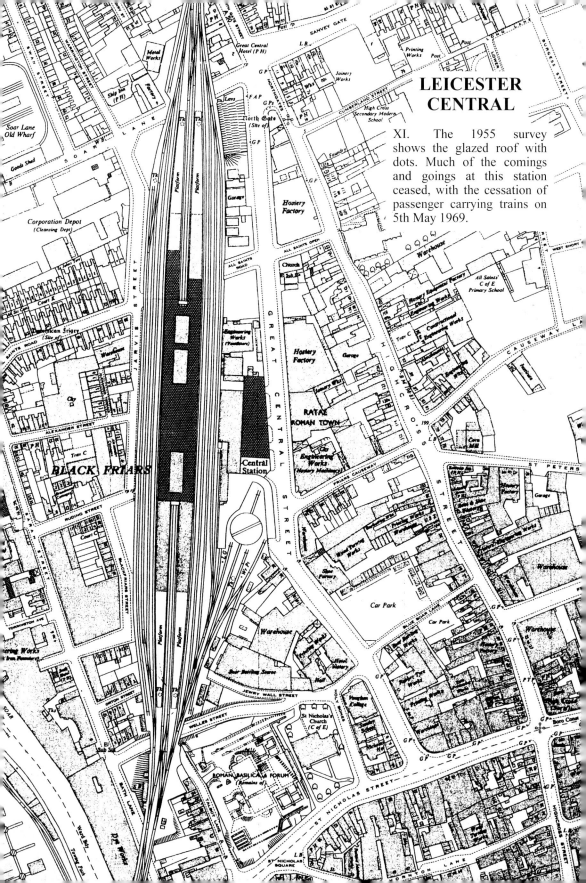

LEICESTER CENTRAL

XI. The 1955 survey shows the glazed roof with dots. Much of the comings and goings at this station ceased, with the cessation of passenger carrying trains on 5th May 1969.

61.   This delightful postcard picture dating from around 1908 shows the original ornate Flemish-style red brick and terracota station façade and clock tower as we face north along Great Central Street. The horse drawn carriages wait outside the main entrance to the glass covered forecourt and cab stands and, on the extreme left, is the entrance to the parcels offices and yard for delivery wagons. (P.Laming coll.)

→ 62.   At the top of the stairs, on the right, the broad expanse of the island platform and its facilities are well illustrated here in this postcard view, again dating from around 1908. Greeting passengers as they surface from street level is the bookstall with its abundance of reading matter to occupy the journey. In amongst the plethora of advertising can be glimpsed finger boards indicating the next train from various platforms. We are looking south along Platform 6 and over to the left a GC 4-4-0 is on pilot duties shunting the parcels dock. Beyond the bookstall the platform buildings contain various waiting rooms and beyond, glimpsed between the columns, a train waits in the south bay Platform 3 for business. (P.Laming coll.)

63.   In the opposite direction, again in about 1908, a southbound express arrives at Platform 6 behind a class GC 4-4-2 No. 264. As we look north the platform buildings containing the refreshment and ladies rooms are evident on the left. Of interest is the signal just above the train, which was controlled by a signal box situated on the platform. In the distance, another set of coaches stand in the north bay Platform 1 awaiting a turn on a northbound local. The plated section to the right of the arriving train indicates the bridge that carries the railway over All Saints Road. (D.C.Pearce coll.)

64.   Moving out from under the canopies to the south end of the station we are looking across the south end bays in the early 1900s. It's lunch-time and standing at Platform 6 is the York to Bournemouth train headed by an interesting combination of a class GC 4-4-0 coupled to a GW Dean single 4-2-2. Great Western engines were by no means uncommon visitors to the station throughout its life working in from Banbury and Oxford, usually on cross-country workings. (P.Laming coll.)

➔ 65. This time entering Platform 4, class 11B 4-4-0 No 1021 brings in a local from the south on 30th July 1910. Also in view are the bay platform starter signals controlled from the Passenger South signal box. They are framed by twin water tanks and columns, there to replenish locos in the bays or at the south end of Platform 6, on the left. In the distance, just to the left of the train, can be seen the large signal gantry that protected the southern approach to the station, perched high above the dye works that divided Bath Lane from the River Soar crossing. To the right of the train is Platform 5. (G.W.Goslin coll.)

➔   66. The scale of things can be gauged by this aerial view taken in the 1930s from the west which shows the elevated position the line cut through the city. The main station buildings are in the centre of the picture fronting onto Great Central Street to the left of the turntable. At the bottom of the picture is the River Soar Navigation. A good impression is gained of the nearly 1300' length of the island platform with its two sets of bay platforms set into it at each end and the main 'through lines' skirting either side. (N.Tout coll.)

67.   Back under the canopy finds local GC 4-4-2 No 5266 on station pilot duties alongside the northbound Platform 5. The hydraulic buffers for the south bay platforms are glimpsed on the right and immediately to the left of the loco is the down passenger loop followed by the down goods loop. An additional siding was provided against the parapet of the viaduct on the extreme left to store spare coaching stock as seen in this mid-1930s view. Passenger activity on the platform suggests the pilot is attaching or detaching a van from a northbound passenger train. (Stations UK)

68.   We are now looking north with Platform 5 or the down through platform on our left. Bay Platform 4 has a parcels van at the buffers, but Platform 3 has Cardiff Canton based class 9F 2-10-0 No 92003 with an up local, probably for Woodford. This view, taken around 1959, also offers a glimpse across Platform 6 of the loco servicing facility near Great Central Street, with GW Hall class 4-6-0 No. 6976 *Graythwaite Hall* in attendance. The prominent signals on the bracket to the right control, on the left, the exit from the up passenger loop and, on the right, the up goods loop. (W.A.Camwell/SLS)

69.   The station is guarded at its south end by the 55-lever Leicester South Passenger signal box seen here. This view looking back from a southbound train in 1966 shows the northbound platform on the left, together with the two south bays and their attendant water columns. The signal box lingered on to the end, closing on the 4th May 1969. (C.Weightman/A.Bullimore coll.)

70.   Looking across Platforms 3 and 6 the loco servicing facilities can be seen near the 70'
turntable in May 1961. Another Banbury based Hall class 4-6-0 No. 6929 *Whorlton Hall* stands
by the water column waiting to take over one of the southbound fish trains, as Woodford based B1
4-6-0 No 61106 waits to work home with an evening southbound local. This picture well illustrates
the nature of Leicester as a staging point for changing engines for many years. With the closure of
the local shed in July 1964, this time honoured tradition ceased.
(6201 Princess Elizabeth Society coll.)

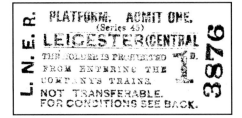

71.   Moving out now to the end of Platform 5, the north end bay platforms, numbers 1 and 2, can be seen on the left. As Black 5 class 4-6-0 No. 44847 departs with the 16.38 Marylebone to Nottingham on this dull August evening in 1966. The melancholia is added to by the site of the lifted loop and siding on the right and the bracket, bereft of its associated signal arms, an indication of former busier times. The water tower was one of six that were provided round the station. (Milepost 92½)

72.   This view looking north in August 1967, shows how all the lines converged to cross the viaduct and away to the north. Prominent in the foreground and framing the scene are the twin water tanks and columns serving Platform 5 on the left and bay Platforms 2 and 1 on the right respectively. Also prominent on the right is the Great Central Hotel which, was on the corner of Northgate Street and Soar Lane. By now the bay platforms are out of use, hence the faces of the colour light signals beyond the water columns are turned away. (N.Tout)

73. Through the entrance gates the airy forecourt and cab waiting area can be seen on the 4th August 1967. Less than a year after closure as a through route and with wholesale staff withdrawals the station had largely become an unstaffed halt! The arch on the left reveals the entrance to the ticket and booking office and the absence of taxis rather reinforces the gloomy despondency accompanying the reduction in services. (N.Tout)

74.   The absence of signs at the booking office windows confirms the sad demise of the station in another view from August 1967. By now prospective passengers have no need of these facilities as only local tickets can be obtained from the conductor-guard on the few remaining trains. The wood panelling is so redolent of Great Central booking offices at the larger stations, reflecting the bold optimism of the Victorian era in which it was installed. (N.Tout)

75.   From the Booking Hall passengers accessed the platforms via a subway seen here on the left. Despite the main entrance being on the eastern side of the station it was also possible to gain access from Jarvis Street to the west. The boarded up entrance in the centre of this picture, again from August 1967, served the goods lift, which surfaced in the centre of the island platform above. (N.Tout)

76.   This view from 4th August 1967, shows a deserted Platform 5 and rationalisation setting in. On the left, the carriage siding and the down goods loop have been removed, and the platform buildings on the right are almost all locked up, the only concessions being the toilets and an inhospitable waiting room. Along the platform, under the canopy, can be seen the former Platform signal box, which stands proud of the line of the rest of the buildings in order to afford signalmen a clear view of operations. The box contained two frames, an east and a west frame, each with 30 levers, but had ceased to be operational by 1908. For many years it became the domain of the Transport Police. (N.Tout)

77.   The trams and horse drawn carriages have long since departed and twenty years have elapsed since it was possible to book through tickets to London and the North by the time this view was taken looking along Great Central Street on the 23rd December 1986. The parcels office on the skyline was set back from the street and overlooked the covered area with glazed roof protecting the cab approach. By now the ornate clocktower and decorated gables have been replaced by a rather utilitarian brick balustrade. The car park just above the street on the left in front of the main building occupies the area where the turntable and locomotive servicing facilities were once situated. (D.C.Pearce)

78.   Above the passenger facilities at street level was the Parcels Office seen here looking north. Great Central Street is to the right and to the left would have been the up through lines. It was served by a short siding and covered platform, though much of the mail and parcels traffic was dealt with on the main platform out of sight to the left. The Flemish style is reflected again in the design of the gable ends in this view taken on the 23rd December 1986. (D.C.Pearce)

79.   It's about quarter past seven on a glorious summer evening in August 1966 and Black 5 4-6-0 No 44984 has arrived at Platform 5 with the 16.38 from Marylebone to Nottingham. We are standing on what was the down goods loop looking south and a good view is afforded of the canopy which stretched over 800' along the platform. To the left of the loco is another view of the platform signal box which, since 1964 when the local engine shed closed, had served as the signing on point for loco crews on the Great Central section. (Milepost 92½)

80.   This view, taken in 1967 shows the skew bowstring bridge over Northgate Street and perched high above the street, the 60-lever North Passenger signal box. In the foreground is a short loco siding trailing in from the left which found much use in the process of changing engines on northbound through services in the past. Trailing in from the right are the connections to the bay platforms as the up line curves away to enter Platform 6. The signal box had not long been closed, having been finally switched out on the 29th January 1967. (C.Weightman/A.Bullimore coll.)

81.   Our final view of the Central Station is from a southbound DMU for Rugby, which is approaching the Northgate Street bridge. The view illustrates the way in which the through lines curve round the outside of the island platform, seen through the girders of the bridge. The prominent remains of the bracket signal in the foreground have found further use at Loughborough protecting the approach from the south. The picture dates from the 25th April 1969, less than a couple of weeks from final closure. (D.C.Pearce)

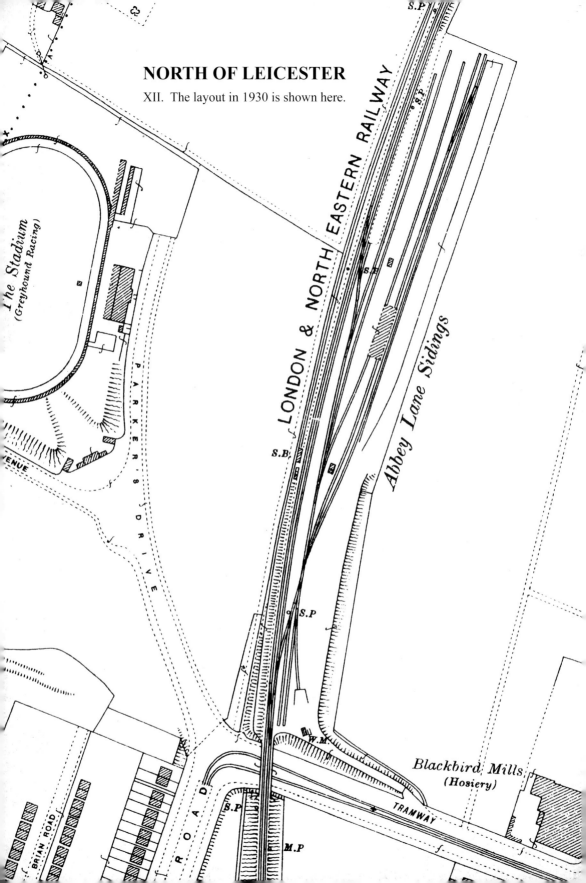

NORTH OF LEICESTER

XII. The layout in 1930 is shown here.

LONDON & NORTH EASTERN RAILWAY

Abbey Lane Sidings

The Stadium
(Greyhound Racing)

PARKER'S DRIVE

VENUE

S.P.

S.B.

S.B.

S.P.

S.P.

W.M.

Blackbird Mills
(Hosiery)

TRAMWAY

ROAD

BRIAN ROAD

S.P.

M.P.

82.   A small coal yard was established, 1584 yards north of Leicester's North Passenger signal box. This view, looking north in 1967, shows the all wooden signal box, typical of those positioned on embankments, with its attendent lamp hut in the foreground. The box contained a 40-lever frame and closed on the 12th May 1968. Over to the right, an oil terminal had been established latterly which regularly took delivery from, amongst other places, Fawley in Hampshire. (C.Weightman/A.Bullimore coll.)

83.   Forging north past the yard on a lovely evening in May 1961 is York B16 4-6-0 No 61461 on its way home with the 18.37 Woodford to Dringhouses fruit and vegetables train. To the left is a glimpse of the coal yard and canopy over the unloading area and, in the distance on the right, the signal box. Coal traffic was usually trip worked from Braunstone Gate goods yard. Although the oil traffic lasted until 1968, coal traffic was withdrawn from the 5th July 1965. (M.Mitchell)

84.   In the opposite direction on the same evening, class K3 2-6-0 No 61813 of Dairycoates
brings the 15.30 Hull to Plymouth fish into Leicester for a booked engine change. As can be seen
in the yard over to the right, the sidings were also used to store surplus coaching stock. By this time
in the evening the signal box would normally be switched out as it was only generally open for
traffic purposes when the yard was to be shunted, usually twice each weekday and once on Saturday
mornings. (M.Mitchell)

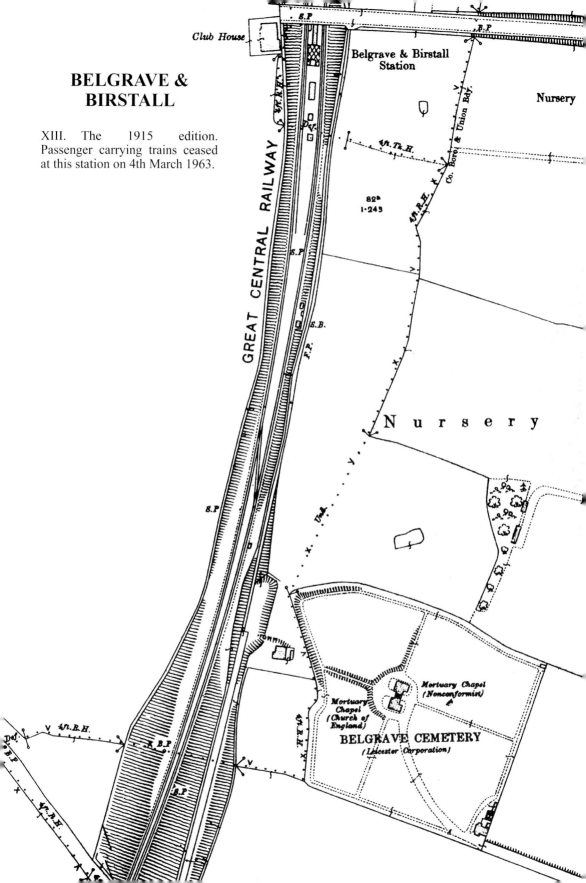

BELGRAVE & BIRSTALL

XIII. The 1915 edition. Passenger carrying trains ceased at this station on 4th March 1963.

Club House

Belgrave & Birstall Station

Nursery

GREAT CENTRAL RAILWAY

Nursery

82ᵇ
1·243

Co. Boro & Union Bdy.

Nursery

BELGRAVE CEMETERY
(Leicester Corporation)

Mortuary Chapel
(Nonconformist)

Mortuary Chapel
(Church of England)

85. We are now looking south from the Station Road bridge on a wet 27th June 1959. 9F 2-10-0 No 92067 is seen in the distance hurrying through with northbound steel empties. The inclement weather will not have found favour with male commuters wishing to avail themselves of the facilities contained in the small building at the far end! Also glimpsed on the left is the signal box and its lamp hut. (Milepost 92½)

86. A closer view, taken from the footpath, seen on the right skirting the east side of the line, shows L1 2-6-4T No 67747 arriving with the 07.40 Nottingham to Rugby local on the 24th July 1961. By now the running-in board, just to the left of the locomotive, is in the corporate maroon livery with the white lettering of the London Midland Region, a take over from the Eastern Region that had been effected from February 1958. The entrance on bridge No.363 from Station Road and the covered stairs leading down to the platform dominate the scene. (M.Mitchell)

87.   1 mile 298 yards north of Abbey Lane was a smaller version of the GC signal box, containing just 18 levers, designed by the Railway Signalling Company, seen here nestling in the side of the shallow cutting. We are looking north in this early 1960s view, with the station beyond. With no goods facilities this was truly a suburban station serving the outskirts of Leicester. (R.K.Blencowe coll.)

88.   Despite suffering the ravages of abandonment and consequent vandalism, the station buildings and island platform lingered long after the station closed on the 4th March 1963. We are looking towards Leicester on the down side of the island with the stairs on the left descending from the road above and the canopy and buildings on the platform remaining more or less intact. This view dates from the 8th April 1973 with track still in situ almost four years after the last trains had passed. (D.C.Pearce)

LEICESTER NORTH

89.   Some fifty years later, the area had undergone something of a transformation as seen in this view looking north on the 25th June 2011. The signalbox had long since gone, having closed on the 13th June 1965, though the recess for it remains on the extreme right in the shallow cutting. The old station was demolished in June 1977, when the buildings became dangerously unsafe. The Great Central Railway preservationists are in the process of establishing a more grandiose southern terminus for the line from Loughborough, the initial phase, providing a new platform, run round loop and siding, seen here. Thus, in 1991, "Leicester North" became the new GC station serving the city. (D.C.Pearce)

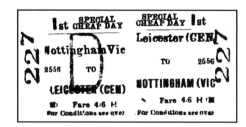

90.   A view looking south and dating from 25th June 2011 illustrates the way in which the old station has made way for the new. Class 8F 2-8-0 No 48305 is departing with a train for Loughborough. Bridge No. 363 carries a cul-de-sac from Loughborough Road, paralleling the railway to the left, to a golf course occupying much of Mowmacre Hill, over to the right. (D.C.Pearce)

91.   From small beginnings in 1969, at the time of closure of the the final remnant of the 'last main line', the Main Line Preservation Group, as it was then known, gathered momentum to establish the present Great Central Railway as a preserved main line. This view looking north on the 25th June 2011 shows the old and new, with the former station entrance bricked up and perched on the bridge as preserved No. 37275 approaches the new platform with a train from Loughborough. The loco itself was just four years old when the line closed! (D.C.Pearce)

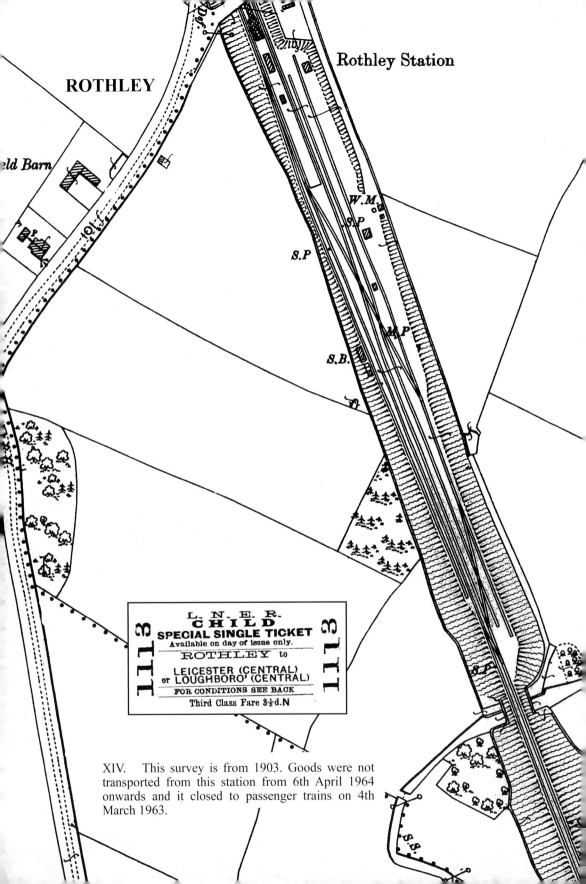

ROTHLEY

Rothley Station

eld Barn

W.M.
S.P

S.P

M.P

S.B.

L. N. E. R.
CHILD
SPECIAL SINGLE TICKET
Available on day of issue only.
ROTHLEY to
LEICESTER (CENTRAL)
or **LOUGHBORO' (CENTRAL)**
FOR CONDITIONS SEE BACK
Third Class Fare 3½d. N

1113   1113

S.P

S.S.

XIV.   This survey is from 1903. Goods were not transported from this station from 6th April 1964 onwards and it closed to passenger trains on 4th March 1963.

92.   The neat and well proportioned layout of the platform buildings are well illustrated here in this period view looking north dating from around 1910. This is the down platform with a trailing connection from the down refuge siding on the left and removed by 1960. Prominent above the station site on the right is the station masters house. (D.C.Pearce coll.)

93.   This early 1900s view also shows the original signal box in the distance which, in common with other boxes on this section of the line, closed on the 13th June 1965. By August 1966 it had been completely razed to the ground. (GCRS)

94.   The station masters house on the right above the station presides over the passage of class V2 2-6-2 No 60918 with the 10am Bradford Exchange to Marylebone on the 22nd August 1959. Also glimpsed on the right is part of the goods yard, which closed on the 6th April 1964. The hoarding on the end of the gents advertises a "Home Life Exhibition". (H.B.Priestley/Milepost 92½)

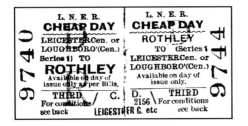

95.   Despite the station closing on the 4th March 1963, the buildings remained remarkably intact, as seen here looking south from the bridge in April 1969. This afternoon working from Rugby to Nottingham Arkwright Street was the final remnant of passenger services and would succumb less than a month later. (Courtney-Haydon coll./RCTS)

96.   We have moved to the up side to see a DMU disappearing in the distance towards Leicester. It also affords us a good view of the remains of the goods yard as the station slumbers during April 1969. On the 8th September 1975 the first passenger train of the preservation era called at the station and regular services to Loughborough resumed in early January 1976. (Courtney-Haydon coll./RCTS)

97.   Bridge No. 354 can be seen in its entirety with the typical station entrance prominent as Black 5 4-6-0 No 45231 prepares to depart with a northbound passenger working on the 16th April 1994. On the up line is the tail end of a goods train in a view which demonstrates the unique qualities of this preserved main line railway. It is not hard to imagine this as an everyday scene from over thirty years earlier before the line closed as a through route. (D.C.Pearce)

98.   Nearly 25 years after initial closure, the station and yard are full of bustle. A carriage and wagon repair shed has been erected towards the far end of the old goods yard and the foliage is noticeably more verdant around the station. Just above the platform buildings on the right is the 'new' 20 lever signal box that came from Blind Lane, near Wembley. N2 0-6-2T No 69523 is running round its train in this view looking south on the 5th June 1988. (D.C.Pearce)

99.   This view looking north on the 25th June 2011 shows the main carriage and wagon repair shed with the station in the distance to the left. It also shows the commencement of the double track section from here to Loughborough, relayed and reinstated over a six year period from 1994 and completed for official opening on the 1st June 2000. (D.C.Pearce)

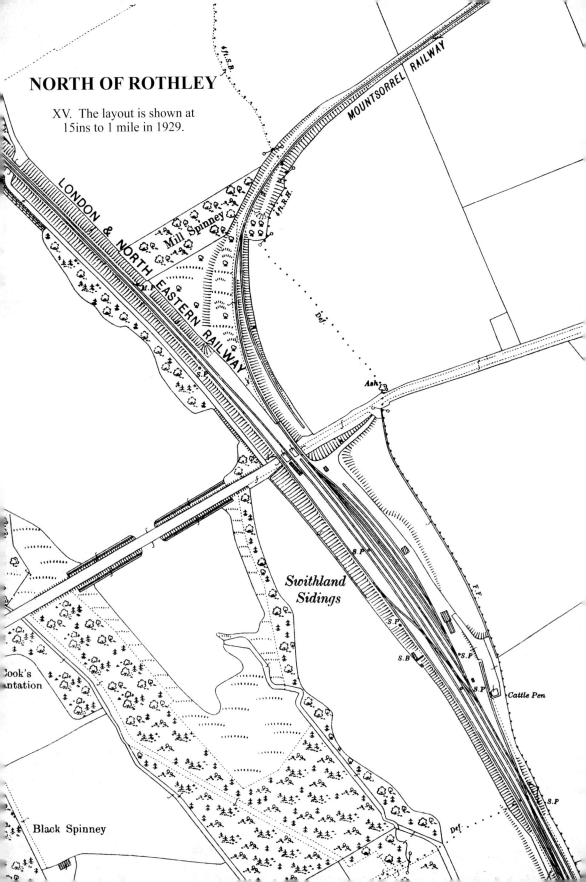

NORTH OF ROTHLEY

XV. The layout is shown at
15ins to 1 mile in 1929.

MOUNTSORREL RAILWAY

LONDON & NORTH EASTERN RAILWAY

Mill Spinney

Ash

Swithland
Sidings

Cook's
antation

Black Spinney

Cattle Pen

S.B

100.   Less than a mile north of Rothley the GC established a small goods yard and exchange sidings for traffic from the Mountsorrel granite quarries, situated to the east of the line. The 40-lever signal box that once controlled the yard was situated on the left of this view looking north but closed on the 13th June 1965. It was demolished shortly afterwards. This was another location that benefitted from wartime improvements in 1941 with the provision of loops. Under preservation, these have been reinstated to provide extra flexibility, as seen here on the 25th June 2011 as the 'new' signalling awaits commissioning. (D.C.Pearce)

101.   The Mountsorrel branch curved away from the main line just to the north of the yard and is itself, in part, subject to a preservation appeal. As we look north on the 25th June 2011 the newly relaid line can be seen curving in to cross bridge No. 352. It began operations in 1861 and was extended to link with the GC in 1898. Traffic ceased around 1959 and the sidings themselves were closed on the 6th April 1964. (D.C.Pearce)

102.   It was originally intended to build a station here and the bridge (No. 352), in the foreground, was duly designed to accommodate a stairwell, the brick arch of which is still visible at street level. As seen in this view looking south the main running lines were also spaced apart to allow room for a platform to be built. A replacement 55-lever signal box can be seen, built on the opposite side of the line from the original, itself recovered from Aylesbury South. (D.C.Pearce)

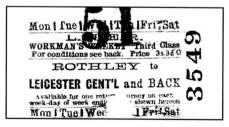

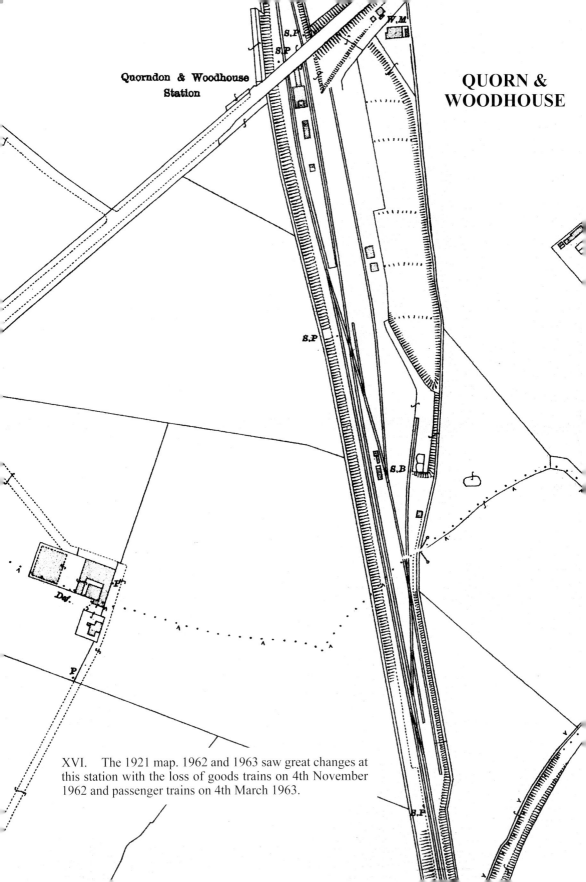

Quorndon & Woodhouse
Station

**QUORN &
WOODHOUSE**

XVI.   The 1921 map. 1962 and 1963 saw great changes at
this station with the loss of goods trains on 4th November
1962 and passenger trains on 4th March 1963.

103.   Up to the early 1950s when this view was taken, the station had ornate lamps and signage. We are looking north along the up platform as a member of the station staff escorts passengers to our waiting train. Again, the arrangement of platform buildings is so redolent of the GC extension's smaller stations, achieving a remarkably consistent uniformity so characteristic of the line. (D.Thompson/Stations UK)

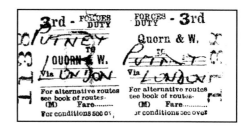

104. The corporate London Midland Region maroon with white lettering is evident on the running-in board as we look north towards bridge No 342 on the down side of the island platform. Glimpsed on the right is the lane that led into the goods yard past the weighbridge in this early 1960s view, together with the up reception loop, another wartime improvement. (Stations UK)

105. The promise of a glorious summer day in July 1961 is demonstrated in this view from bridge No 342 looking south. It offers another glimpse of the goods yard, over to the left, as a BR Standard class 5 4-6-0 arrives with an early morning northbound local train. The station has less than two years left as part of the BR network, closing on the 4th March 1963. (M.Mitchell)

106.   The view north on the 15th August 1964 affords a glimpse of the goods yard and associated buildings over to the right as a rebuilt 'Jubilee' 4-6-0 No 45735 *Comet* brings the 13.23 (Saturdays Only) Skegness to Leicester train on the last leg of its journey. The white building just above the loco was the former station masters house, and the trackless yard bears witness to the withdrawal of the goods facilities on the 4th November 1963. (D.Holmes)

107.   The sultry summer Saturday afternoon of the 15th August 1964 finds V2 2-6-2 No 60976 steadily heading north past the 40 lever signal box with the 10.45 (Saturdays Only) Poole to Sheffield Victoria train. The box closed on the 13th June 1965 and was subsequently demolished. (D.Holmes)

108.   An intial attempt to operate a service between Loughborough and Quorn began in the autumn of 1973 but had to be suspended pending the granting of a Light Railway Order. Black 5 4-6-0 No 5231 sets off back to Loughborough on the 28th October 1973 and one wonders what the Health and Safety Executive would make of the gentleman carrying out some repointing work on bridge 342. The arched window on the left was for a storeroom that led from the porters room accessed from the down platform. (D.C.Pearce)

109.   Despite this being a view of the trackless down platform in August 1981, it illustrates the care that has been taken in restoring the canopy and platform buildings. Track was relaid at this platform during 1985 and by 2000 had become part of the double track main line the preservationists had aspired to in 1969. (D.C.Pearce)

110.   Something of the determination of the Main Line Preservation Group can be gauged from this picture looking north in 1982. BR had removed the down line in July 1976 leaving just the former up line as the only link between Loughborough and Rothley. However, by now the group had turned itself into the Great Central Railway Company (1976) Ltd with credibility enough to be entrusted with such locos as the Stirling Single 4-2-2 No 1, on loan from the NRM, seen here with a southbound train. (D.C.Pearce)

111.   The view looking south from the end of the platform in June 2011 shows something of a renaissance. The double track and down refuge siding on the right have been restored and the 'new' 29 lever signal box seen on the left, recovered from Market Rasen and erected in 1987, was commissioned in 2004. The turntable from York (Queen Street) was installed here on 9th September 2011. (D.C.Pearce)

112.   This view on the up side in February 1992 shows the covered stairway down from the street entrance on Woodhouse Road/Forest Road. At the bottom of the stairs passengers remained, more or less, in the dry as they passed the combined station nameboard and advertising hording before attending at the booking office on the left. The chimney adjacent to the street entrance top right served the porters' room situated under the stairs. (D.C.Pearce)

SOUTH OF LOUGHBOROUGH

113.   We are looking north from bridge No.338 which carries Woodthorpe Road over the railway. The bridge in the distance (No.337) carries the A6 from Loughborough to Leicester in a view that will be very familiar to many who frequent the line today. Taken in the mid 1930s this view shows B1 (later B18) class 4-6-0 No 5196 with the Newcastle to Swansea making steady progress south in the early afternoon. (D.C.Pearce coll.)

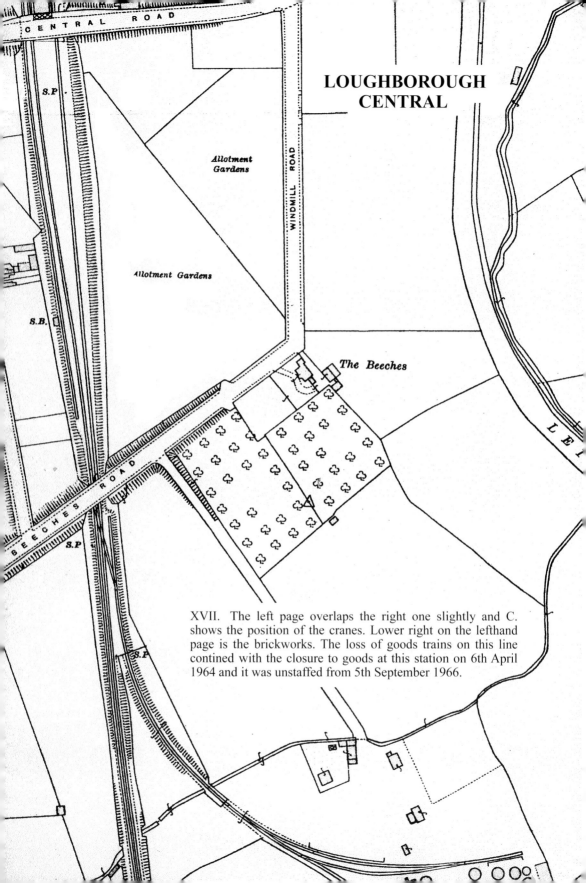

LOUGHBOROUGH CENTRAL

CENTRAL ROAD

S.P.

Allotment Gardens

WINDMILL ROAD

Allotment Gardens

S.B.

The Beeches

BEECHES ROAD

S.P.

S.P.

L E I

XVII. The left page overlaps the right one slightly and C. shows the position of the cranes. Lower right on the lefthand page is the brickworks. The loss of goods trains on this line contined with the closure to goods at this station on 6th April 1964 and it was unstaffed from 5th September 1966.

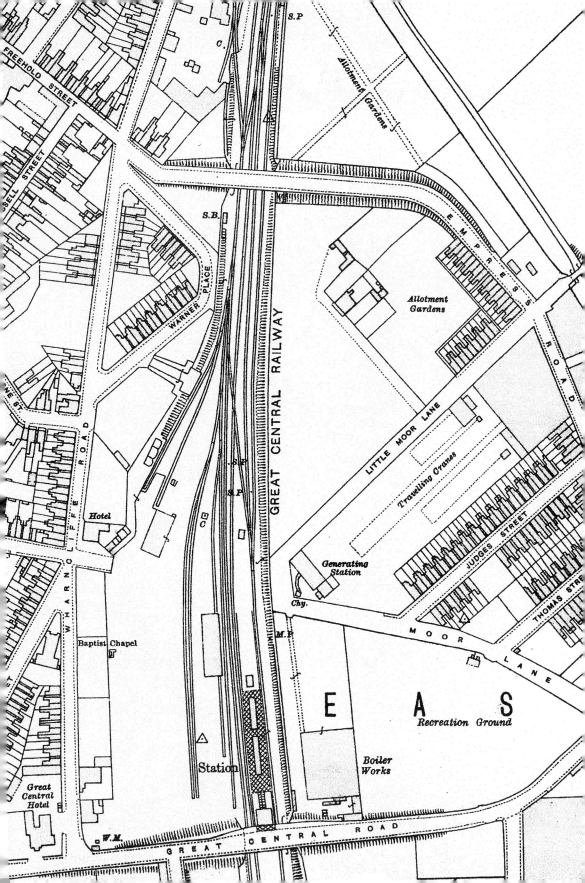

114.　This photograph from Great Central Road in the mid 1950s, offers a view of the yard, together with the more substantial platform buildings seen on the down side to the right. The goods yard ceased operations on the 6th April 1964 and was subsequently given over to industrial use. (D.Thompson/Stations UK)

115.　Viewed from the down platform on 29th April 1956, class A3 4-6-2 No 60102 *Sir Frederick Banbury* approaches with an afternoon express for Marylebone. The elaborate 'running in board' was replaced in 1958 by a slightly more utilitarian maroon sign sporting the legend 'Loughborough Central'.　(Milepost 92½)

116.   Looking across Great Central Road a close view is afforded of the station entrance and circulating area. As befits a large town, the station building is slightly more elaborate with the ticket office windows and the booking office at street level rather than down on the platform as at smaller stations. The picture was taken on the 3rd May 1969, the last day of the train service between Nottingham and Rugby. (D.C.Pearce)

117.   At this time the double track was still in situ and Manning Wardle 0-6-0ST *Littleton No.5* trundles in from Quorn on the 28th October 1973, four days after delivery from the Foxfield Railway. In common with many of the other stations on the route, rationalisation around 1965 had resulted in the loops, installed in 1941, being removed and a tremendous air of decay descending upon the line. (D.C.Pearce)

118.   We are looking south along the up platform towards bridge No.333 in 1970. Noticeable is the substantial length of the station canopy and the more generously proportioned gentlemen's toilet this end of the platform. Although the weeds are beginning to take over, the white edging to the platform still remains as a warning to the unwary. Over to the right can be glimpsed light industrial units in the fenced off goods yard. (D.C.Pearce coll.)

119.   The view from the Beeches Road (formerly Windmill Road) bridge No.334 looking north offers dramatic views of departing trains as they burst out from under bridge No.333 seen in the distance. At one time, on the left, there was a South signal box that controlled rail access to Messrs Tuckers' brick and tile works situated to the east of the line just south of bridge No.334. Black 5 4-6-0 No 5231 departs with the Wirral Society's 'Great Central Special' on the 4th December 1976. (D.C.Pearce)

120.   Viewed this time from below Beeches Road in June 2011, the station booking hall is prominent on Great Central Road. The line has much more of a businesslike appearance about it with the double track restored, together with loops and sidings, a tribute to all those who set out to preserve something of the GC in 1969. (D.C.Pearce)

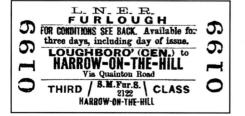

MP Middleton Press

EVOLVING THE ULTIMATE RAIL ENCYCLOPEDIA

Easebourne Lane, Midhurst, West Sussex.
GU29 9AZ   Tel:01730 813169
www.middletonpress.co.uk   email:info@middletonpress.co.uk
A-978 0 906520   B- 978 1 873793   C- 978 1 901706   D-978 1 904474
E- 978 1 906008   F- 978 1 908174

All titles listed below were in print at time of publication - please check current availability by looking at our
website - *www.middletonpress.co.uk* or by requesting a Brochure which includes our
LATEST RAILWAY TITLES also our TRAMWAY, TROLLEYBUS, MILITARY and WATERWAYS series